YiKES!

I'VE GOT TO GET A JOB

6 Steps to an Effective Job Search

YiKES!

I'VE GOT TO GET A JOB

Gain Competitive Advantage in Your Job Search

Reduce Anxiety by Covering All the Bases

A Linear Process that Will Last Your Entire Career

MATT OSTROFSKY

Published by Linear Career Solutions, LLC
www.linearcareersolutions.com

To contact the author about speaking, workshops or ordering books in bulk, email matt@linearcareersolutions.com

ISBN 979-8-9887315-0-4 (paperback)
ISBN 979-8-9887315-1-1 (ebook)

Editor: David Aretha
Book designer: Jerry Dorris, AuthorSupport.com
Book consultant: Martha Bullen, Bullen Publishing Services

Printed in the United States of America

CONTENTS

- Lists common questions to prepare for *and* questions the candidate should have for the interviewer
- Reinforces that this is a two-way process—prospective employees need to interview the employer

- Confirms that receiving an offer begins a potential negotiation
- Suggests a benign approach to gain value—though not everyone is willing to try

- Introduces networking as the #1 element of a job search and how to overcome fear or embarrassment
- Walks the reader through the process from turning a networking call from a cry for help to an offer to help!
- Offering to help others provides a big payoff—sharing what you learned in your job search. *You too can help!*

- Covers my career progression from manufacturing into sales as an example of critically evaluating and connecting my interests, passion, and aspirations
- Explains why I wrote *Yikes!* and how everyone can make a positive impact by offering of themselves to those in a job search

- Websites, suggested books, and related links and QR codes

- Example resumes (good and bad), marketing briefs, and reference lists

Why I wrote this book

You lost your job. Maybe the company was downsized. Possibly, it just was not a good fit. Now what? You are out of work. No pay. No access to health benefits. No 401K contribution. Maybe you were given a severance, have filed for unemployment compensation, and are paying COBRA-level healthcare premiums. You have numerous bills pouring in like the mortgage, car payments, utilities, cell phone plan, internet, auto and homeowners insurance, music lessons, and even pets to feed! Ugh!

To complicate matters, you have not maintained your resume in years. You use LinkedIn to track old friends and check on past loves but have not updated your profile in years. Your professional network is small and stale. You are confused, anxious, and irritated. Now what?

Do not feel bad. Your reactions are perfectly understandable. The intent of this book is to focus you on an effective and efficient path to a new career opportunity. I speak from experience, knowing that you are covering all the bases, will help you sleep at night and lower your stress level.

I was in a similar situation in 2010 after a downsizing. Through an "out of the blue" referral—what my friends and I call a "God moment"—I was introduced to a "job-seeker" group. I never knew volunteer-led job-seeker groups existed. I learned from listening to and applying what the volunteers shared. I was so grateful that I became a volunteer after landing a job. One thing led to another ... and now you are reading this book. Like I did, you came to the realization: *Yikes! I've got to get a job.*

It is quite a helpless feeling being out of work. That feeling gets compounded by not knowing what to do next. This book outlines a structured **6-Step Process** designed to give you peace of mind through the ordeal. All you have to do is follow the process. You will learn and improve your skills.

The **6-Step Process** is a step-by-step guide that brings order and confidence during this stressful time. Following the process will help you work in a smart and linear, focused manner. You will leverage dozens of ideas and decades' worth of experience. In this book, numerous tips and tricks are explained, which optimize time, create competitive advantage, and provide you with confidence in a job search. All gained firsthand as I've made helping people in your situation my "life's mission." I have helped hundreds people so far.

Job searching is not easy. It can be stressful to deal with rejection. However, it is an iterative learning process. You will be much more effective from practice and the experiences you will go through. As with many things in the twenty-first century, there is a "science" to most aspects of the process. These phenomena are explained and clarified. You will learn the right skills and how to apply them to your advantage. Think of it this way, the resume or your LinkedIn profile gets the phone call, the phone call gets the interview, the interview gets an offer, and the offer is your one chance to establish your baseline salary and benefits package. And most everything in an offer is negotiable.

Finally, as an added bonus, you will be better prepared should you be downsized again. Unfortunately, this is a real possibility. As an "at-will" employee, you can be released (i.e., fired) without cause. For no reason whatsoever. Just as you can leave your employer for a better position whenever opportunity strikes. So, keeping your network active by helping others is beneficial to you and those you help!

Keep looking up!

Matt Ostrofsky

INTRODUCTION TO THE 6-STEP PROCESS

The **6-Step Process** begins in "Step 1: Career and Skills Assessment" to help you understand the value of what you bring to market. You will define and list your experiences, competencies, and skills. We discuss career direction ideas there as well.

In "Step 2: The Resume," together, we develop a great resume. I follow a tried-and-true format that is friendly to the latest screening technologies. It will be designed and written to motivate human resource (HR) job screeners to call you. I'll educate you on how to connect the resume to the job description. This compels them to want to call you. You will be packaged as a highly qualified candidate. Proper resume writing increases the odds of you getting a "phone screen" call, the precursor to an online (i.e. Teams Call) or in-person interview. The interview is your opportunity to earn an offer.

After writing your resume, the natural progression leads to "Step 3: LinkedIn and Applying Online." Tips will be provided on how to optimize your LinkedIn profile. Then we will address best practices on how to apply online. LinkedIn is the number-one website searched to find talent. Whether you like social media or not, a professional profile on this site is a must for mid-career, white-collar job search. We also address many of the time-wasting "traps" of applying online.

Next is "Step 4: Phone Screens and Interviews," where you will be coached on how to prepare for and execute them. This step will teach you methods to help you dramatically improve your effectiveness. Concepts on proper preparation and execution are outlined. At the top of the list is the critical skill of knowing how to research target companies and employees, past and present, to gain valuable insights. Questions to prepare for and questions to ask are introduced and discussed. Step four concludes with follow-up procedures and timing.

An important aspect of the job search flows through the first steps, which involve the critical review of your background and career objectives. They must align with any job [description] you pursue. You must genuinely meet the bulk of the requirements and qualifications. Your probability of success increases as your alignment with the needs of the open position improves. Conversely, you are better off searching for a better fit than applying to a position and then hoping to get a call.

"Step 5: Negotiating an Offer" follows with tips on how to accept and negotiate a job offer. Steps are listed on how to politely ask for additional compensation. Clearly, sensitivity to your financial situation and comfort with asking should be considered. You will be surprised how a focused approach can increase a sign-on bonus or lead to additional time off and/or some other benefit. This is your lone opportunity to establish your baseline compensation—a critical part of onboarding.

Finally, in "Step 6: Networking and Helping Others," the critical nature of networking is reinforced. It is the number-one thing you must do in your job search. Speak with industry friends and associates on the phone. It is the part of your search where you connect with anyone who knows you and what you can do. Advise them that you are looking for an opportunity. People are most comfortable reaching out to former managers or subordinates where you have realized success. However, clients, vendors, division managers, and general managers all the way to presidents are potential connections—to opportunities. Friends from your Y, church, and neighborhood can help too.

There is a goal to the **6-Step Process:** The big payoff. Once you land, you circle back and thank anyone who helped you. Update anyone you contacted. Share the good news! You shift the nature of the call from an *appeal for help* to an *offer to help!* A great reason for a call. This is the big payoff!

There are a lot of people looking for work. Searching for a better opportunity. People are aware of others who are looking. Offering to help now makes it easier to stay in touch and maintain your network. You will learn to *enjoy* networking with this mindset.

The most rewarding part of networking is getting to know and helping others.

Frankly, it is why I wrote *Yikes!* A satisfying, pleasant sensation or natural high can be obtained from helping someone in the throes of job loss. It can be very profound. Discussing something as critical as someone's career, giving good advice, and making connections with them can be spiritual. I find it life-fulfilling and think you will too! Sharing one or two ideas you learned can help someone else optimize their search!

What Is a Job Search?

Let us start with the basics. What is a job? It is a set of measurable deliverables that create economic value. When it becomes cost-effective for an employer to pay someone to do the work—*bam*—a job is created! The challenge in your job search is to let the prospective employer know you can deliver the results.

How do you find jobs? It may be obvious to use Google, Indeed.com, TheLadders.com, or a myriad of other websites, and of course, you can find many jobs listed on company websites under "careers" or "employment opportunities." There are also listings in trade associations by industry and in the hard-copy Sunday paper of any major market. There are also resources you can access through web applications. One such site, specialized to college graduates, is Handshake. This site connects students and graduates with organizations that recruit from their educational institution. They post jobs, and the school's career placement and career advancement teams can help with the student's application. For that matter, any mid-career job-seeker would be wise to re-engage with their undergrad or graduate college or university's career advancement department. They are very good resources for early or mid-career job-seekers, folks looking for a second career, or people late in their career in search of consulting opportunities.

One aspect of job search is accurately describing your experiences and skills in a package. It is done with a compelling and impactful document—the resume. It is best when the resume is aligned to a specific job. Jobs are defined by a "Job Description." These include criteria described with unique "keywords." Keywords are selected and used to describe the type of experiences, skills, and education the employer deem necessary for success. Though some job descriptions may be out of date, addressing what is spelled out in the description is your best way to be considered—to pass the screening filters and get a phone call.

There is a critical aspect to the job search many people gloss over. It is essential to critically evaluate how well your experience and skills meet the defined requirements. They are called requirements for a reason. The greater the alignment and match of your background to the requirements, the more likely you are to be considered. You want the chance to tell your story, but you have to be qualified to have a chance. Therefore, critical evaluation and self-reflection are a must. You must be self-aware. Many people, myself included, have fallen into the trap of taking "long shots" at job opportunities. This can be discouraging. You <u>must</u> have the right qualifications to be considered.

There are a few instances when applying to jobs where your alignment is low makes sense but only as a calculated risk. It takes precious time and energy to apply. One such exception is to get into a target company's database. Ultimately, you may be great for another position you have not reviewed or one that is not posted yet. This scenario can occur, but the odds are low.

Along the way, I'll highlight some important points to consider with the "Yikes! Nugget" banner. For example, here is the first nugget—you will need a reliable word processing platform. There are "Yikes! Assignments" throughout the **6-Step Process** too!

YiKES! NUGGET

Invest in Your Personal Computing Platform

If you have been released mid-career and have not upgraded your personal laptop in years, now is the time to do so. Many people currently use their company laptop and virtual private network (VPN) to work remotely. If this is you, please consider investing in a:

- Laptop or a desktop
- Software

- Security software
- Backup process
- Personal VPN
- Printer (3-in-1 printer, scanner, and copier—some have fax capability too)

Stay with high-quality products but shop and learn. You should consider nothing less than a computer with an "8 gigabyte" (8GB) hard-drive. Low-price printers can cost a fortune to operate once you factor in the expensive toner cartridges. You'll need to print copies of your resume to have during interviews and for networking events – so a printer will be necessary. You may best research this on-line or visit Best Buy for some assistance – I've found their sales techs to be very knowledgeable.

It is best to use the Microsoft Office Suite with Word, Excel, and PowerPoint. You will need all three. Word and Excel are needed for resume writing. PowerPoint, used for creating presentations (a "slide deck"), is also required on some interviews. VPN service is available from your internet provider or third party. Do some research but *please make the move to secure your system and employ a backup routine!*

For example, a marketing manager using the Yikes! process was asked to create a marketing plan for a product launch. He was asked to make this presentation in a late-round interview. This is a reasonable request—and a great opportunity to illustrate value for the position. He drafted it in PowerPoint. Our job-seeker volunteers and I reviewed the presentation for content and flow. Also, he practiced presenting it with our group. He was confident. He aced the presentation and advanced through the process.

You will need a good, cost-effective printer. The Hewlett Packard (HP) family of OfficeJet three-in-one printers are reliable; however, they can be expensive to operate. Toner cartridges are relatively expensive. For black and white resume and cover letter printing, you would be fine with an Epson EcoTank or an HP printer. Research what you need but get reliable printing capability (find the data on the cost per page). Your resume will evolve and improve over time. You will need copies available for interviews, job-seeker meetings, and networking events. You will print documents often in job search.

Those in the arts, advertising, and education industries will need industry-appropriate software. Apple (Mac) hardware and software are suitable if not necessary. In good old industrial manufacturing, where I grew up, we used personal computers (PC systems) and Microsoft products. Keep in mind Mac's are more costly and make-up less than 15% of the market. Give a lot of thought of going in a new computing direction as job search will be stressful enough – you don't need the complications of struggling learning the idiosyncrasies of a new computing platform.

Finally, make sure you have security software, a backup system, and a good Virtual Private Network (VPN) for keeping things secure. You will be online a lot, and you will not have the luxury of your former employer's IT Support "Help Desk" and firewall systems. You do not want a virus or malware destroying your system. Also, it is recommended to never click on a link embedded in an email from an address you do not know, recognize, or trust. They can launch destructive malware or worse viruses that can destroy your computer. I'm no IT expert, however, Andy Geremia a friend and work associate, suggests the low-cost tools such as a Google Chromebook and their free gmail email accounts which can include a free automatic back-up with the Gdrive feature. Microsoft has a 365 Plan that allows you to use the Office tools in a browser. Some of these tools can be accessed for free from a computer you would access in a library too. Some avenues to consider.

Speaking of "infrastructure," here is a nugget to improve your professional reputation in your job search.

YiKES! NUGGET

Use a Personalized Voicemail Greeting

Please add a personal greeting to your cell phone voicemail. This courtesy will ensure that people who do not have your number saved know they've reached you. A small, if not subliminal sign, that you are a professional.

You can personalize your voicemail greeting by accessing the voicemail button on your cell phone. Once in your voicemail menu, select "Greeting." You will then be given the option of recording a custom greeting. I recommend you simply state your name. You do not need a rambling message such as, "Hello, you have reached Sam Dillard's cell phone. I am unable to answer the phone now. Leave your name, number, and a brief message. I'll call you as soon as I am able. And please, make it a great day!" They know what to do and whether they've reached you. Those types of greetings are not necessary and waste time. Simply state your name loud and clear. This is handy even when people do not leave a voicemail as it confirms they have the correct number. They may now choose to text you. You will make their day great by returning their call! Should you want to leave a more personalized message, do so quickly. Be respectful of the caller's time.

The Big Payoff

Beyond getting a new job, the **6-Step Process** will help you understand the importance of networking—*the most important aspect* of a job search and a skill to be developed over time. Ultimately, when you land your new role, as outlined in "Step 6: Networking and Helping Others," you will be guided on how to thank the folks who have helped you. Part of this step is to offer your assistance should anyone in your network need help someday. Maybe those you contact know others in need of help. Heck, they may have recently downsized or terminated people from their team. Offering to share some tips and time with them will certainly endear you to them!

I know that when I'm engaged in helping others in their job search, I'm in a great place physically, mentally, and spiritually. No bad thoughts, no wasted time. It is where the good Lord wants us to operate. Giving of ourselves to help others!

The psychic income—or "feel good" stuff that fills your brain and body—makes the effort satisfying. This process will naturally lead you to adopt this mindset. The **6-Step Process** concludes with a profound realization: You have learned a lot about the process, and you are now able to help others.

The **6-Step Process** is based on personal and professional experiences and insights. These tips and ideas came from my experiences with people who have focused all or part of their career on a professional, college-educated career track. Often referred to as white-collar professions, these jobs require a resume—or a curriculum vitae (CV) in the education or research fields—when applying for a position. There is much emphasis on the resume as, in the United States, it is the commonly accepted and most often-requested job-seeker document. There is an alternate layout, known by some as a marketing brief or a "one-pager", used in special circumstances that we will discuss in detail in "Step 2: The Resume."

Today, even when applying to many blue-collar jobs (service jobs, vocational-skilled, or unskilled labor), the creation of a resume is a necessity. A resume organizes your career progression. It records your body of work and defines the impact you have made in these jobs or assignments. Another bonus to the resume is that you can present your background in a chronological, easy-to-read manner to help speed up the completion of an application. Turning in a resume with a job application, even for a part-time job, will position you in a better light. It is a professional move that can inspire a prospective employer to think of you beyond their immediate need. You plant the seed for advancement to a supervisory role—or a transition from blue-collar to white-collar work. Exactly what I did upon graduating college. I was a mechanic one day and then a production control/shipping and receiving supervisor the next!

Additionally, capturing your work history in an organized manner can help when discussing your background with counselors. A resume might be required by some hiring managers or a human resources department anyway, so there is value in developing one. Even factory labor, lab tech work, skilled trade, or other blue-collar positions may require a resume. I'm here to tell you—developing and writing your resume is of benefit. It will not only help you find employment, but as your career develops, it will also become a "living document" upon which can you build for the duration of your career. In a weird way, resumes are interesting references for family members who may someday want to write a eulogy about you. Yes, odd—and maybe even morbid—but true.

One of the lessons detailed in this book is derived from my ability to "channel" numerous encounters throughout my career. I've crafted these ideas, concepts, and techniques from my experiences with recruiters, volunteers, and HR personnel. Strong references will be invaluable during your job search. I've met and networked with them and read and listened to their presentations, and I can now pass that knowledge on to you. Many have coached me over the years, and a myriad of their ideas have been included to help you through this stressful time. Never forget—you are a one-in-a-million gift from God! You have accumulated unique experiences while growing up, in school, and throughout your career "body of work." All of which are unique to you. Be proud of what you bring to market. You have great value to the right employer!

The process is not perfect. Circumstances and situations are always dynamic ... subject to change for seemingly no logical reason. I will make recommendations you may choose not to utilize. It is your choice, but keep in mind that the more of the **6-Step Process** you follow, the greater your chances of success will be. The goal is to find a good situation as quickly as possible.

Read the Complete Book First—Then Start the Process

You should read or quickly scan the book completely first to get an overview of the **6-Step Process.** The process is iterative. You will learn and become more proficient over time. Research, preparation, and practicing the steps will pave the way to success. Reading the holistic overview first will help you—then dig in!

An effective job search requires the right frame of mind. Job searching is a full-time job. That is true for a recent college grad or a thirty-year veteran. The same rules apply if you are just out of school, recently downsized, or looking for a new set of challenges. Opportunities for growth and better compensation are out there. However, it is important to know that *this will take time.* The old cliché fits: "It's a marathon, not a sprint." Patience is a virtue.

You will want to pace yourself and understand that there will be lean times in your search. Days or weeks may pass, and opportunities will go cold or stop. It will become frustrating if not depressing at various moments. Hence, you have to be disciplined. Pace yourself. Keep perspective. You have unique interests and a one-in-a-million set of experiences, competencies, and skills. There is market need. You bring value. Finding the right opportunities takes time. Discovering opportunities where your "package" is appropriately appreciated—in a positive, nurturing culture with a compensation plan you can live with—won't happen immediately. But it will happen. It may take weeks, months, or longer. Stay strong!

During your job search, you will have rough patches during which the interest level is low, your search activity will seemingly not be paying off, and frankly, there will be rejections. They may be numerous. You will learn to understand the value of them. The bright side of more rejections is that they are evidence that you are learning what a job search is all about. You have to be interviewed to advance. Most applicants get rejected. Think about that. The **6-Step Process** accelerates your understanding of an effective job search.

While writing this book, I was blessed with the notion of "core values" by Dr. David Hammonds of Valley Creek Baptist Church in Sharpsburg, Georgia. After one sermon, I realized Dr. David is a special guy. I scheduled time to meet with him to discuss the concept of a book designed to help people in their job search. He liked the idea and shared his career and some values that have motivated him to keep preaching into his seventies. We spent a couple of hours together, and it is my pleasure to share his insights with you.

Dr. David suggested beginning the process with what guides me. My core values. I stressed that my ideas are rooted in the Christian principles of helping others. He had the great suggestion to make the book a "workbook," something people could use and reuse when starting or managing their careers. I took his advice to heart, and a process came to mind. I tip my cap to Dr. David for his inspiration and guidance!

This workbook, therefore, includes several "Yikes! Assignments." These require self-reflection and action. In the beginning, you will need to define your core values. *What drives and inspires you?* To understand where I'm coming from, here are mine:

Core Values:

- Every life has value—we are all gifts from God.
- Everyone has unique life experiences and a valuable skill set—no matter how large or small you may think your skills are, they DO have market value.
- Everyone is responsible for developing their skills for themselves and for

others—those they love. Learning something can never be taken away from you. You cannot unlearn how to ride a bike.

- Everyone should appreciate their skills and offer to share their experiences to help others.

I really believe and value these principles. And I consider it a blessing to have the drive to share them. I've helped many people and have seen the **6-Step Process** work. Additionally, I remain loyal and love God, my wife, my family, and my country!

Therefore, let us get into the first assignment. Define your core values! What do you believe in? What are you striving to do with your life? Take some time to think this through and then write those values down. It may take some time. These may be ideas you've never given voice to and, therefore, they may be challenging to define. You will find the process introspective and enlightening—if not fun. This technique will create a foundation for future Yikes! Assignments. Have fun!

Yikes! ASSIGNMENT 1

Define Your Core Values

Define your four core values—the essence of your purpose. What principles guide you? Your behavior?

1. _____

2. _____

3. _____

4. _____

Gratefulness!

Another aspect of getting into the "right frame of mind" for a job search is gratitude. An inspirational pastor, Jim Donavon, whom I had the pleasure of hearing preach at the Legacy Community Church in Senoia, Georgia, made a strong case for being *grateful*. He emphasized how humans tend to look at things with a "glass half full" mentality or with the sense of feeling put-upon, thinking, "Why me?" Looking for work after a termination can put people in a lonely mindset of "aggrievement and desperation." Jim's remedy for this state of mind is to identify what makes you grateful. When I heard this, I knew it would be applicable to those seeking work.

Think back through your life. Again, be prepared to write down ten people or things for which you are grateful. When I did so, it was very satisfying! It must have released endorphins—those chemicals in the brain that provide a sense of euphoria, of positivity. This enabled me to catch my breath and realize how fortunate I was in so many ways. Sure, I've got issues, problems, concerns, and things to improve—who doesn't? However, the positive response I got from thinking about and writing down the ten things I was grateful for was therapeutic. It has proven supportive and helpful in my life. Keep the list close in difficult times and at the forefront of your mind. It is like a good hug! Always remember—you are a one-in-a-million!

I believe writing down and keeping close the ten things you are grateful for is more than just a job-search-process step. It is not in the **6-Step Process**, however, it is an attitude-altering approach to life I truly hope you embrace. It has helped me. We all have issues to face and difficulties to manage. Never lose sight of what makes you grateful. Share these with friends and family. It has impacted me favorably. Each time I review the list, things just get a little better. The situation gets a little brighter, and my attitude improves. Positivity is good for the soul!

Better times are sure to come in your job search. Keep the list handy and refer to it often.

Now it's time for your second Yikes! Assignment.

YiKES! ASSIGNMENT 2

Write Down 10 Things You are Grateful For

These people, places, experiences, and ideas make your life fulfilling. They make you realize you are meaningful, important, and blessed (4 to 6 minimum, but really give this a lot of consideration):

1. _____

2. _____

3. _____

4. _____

5. _____

6. _____

7. _____

8. _____

9. _____

10. _____

Keep this list handy and think about it often. It will help you keep perspective during the highs and lows of your job search. You will be fine! Okay, back to the situation at hand—you need a job! Let's get the party started!

YiKES! NUGGET

Call and Speak with People Who Know What You Can Do

The number-one thing *you must do* to make your job search effective is to speak with people who know you and what you can do!

History has taught me that staying connected to business associates, even in an occasional sense, is a means to new employment opportunities. An occasional phone call, text exchange, Christmas card, or email exchange will keep a relationship alive. It may be difficult for some, but networking is a skill to learn and improve. Make the time. Networking has made my life a lot more fun and fulfilling.

The key to your job search is letting your network know you are in the market. Remember, these are your professional business associates and some may be friends too. Get comfortable saying, "I was downsized," or, "I was let go due to business economics, and my job was eliminated." This is commonplace. High-performing people are often simply let go due to no fault of their own.

I like the approach (using an sports analogy) of saying "I am a 'free agent' looking for a new team" or "I'm back on the market looking for a new opportunity." Also, do not plan to call everyone in your network immediately (in the first week of your search). Start with a few per day. You will find getting them on the phone a challenge. It may take a few attempts. When you do have that discussion, be honest and get the ball in play. You should give them the option to think about your comments, so let them choose a quiet time when they don't feel rushed to field your phone call—and let them formulate a thoughtful answer. After you get to the main point of the conversation—"I'm a free agent looking for a new team, a new opportunity"—they will likely respond with, "I'm sorry to hear that. Let me see what I can do. It was good to hear from you, and I'll keep you in mind. I'll call if I hear of anything." To which you can thank them and ask if they know of any companies hiring in your area of expertise or if they have a recruiter you could contact. This is known as asking for a referral.

Then, wrap up the call quickly and professionally. Tell them you will keep them apprised of your progress and will stay in touch. And make sure to do just that as time passes. Leave them your cell number before the call ends. Should they have ideas or ask for your resume, you can certainly send the generic version to them.

Below are some additional ideas to consider when making initial networking calls:

- If your job was eliminated or you were fired, do not worry—this is just a career bump in the road.
- Downsizing is just a business decision—you are not alone!
- Awesome, effective, valuable, and productive people are downsized or lose their jobs—it happens daily. The stigma of losing a job is currently low if not nonexistent.
- You are a "free agent"—use this sports analogy to put the idea in play when you speak with others. It will take the edge off the topic.
- When reaching out to people, even if you only leave a voicemail, make it positive. Let them know you are "available for a new assignment—a 'free agent.'" Ask them to keep you in mind if they hear of any job openings and include your cell number. Ask if they know an industry specific recruiter you could contact. At the end of the call, say your cell number slowly and repeat it a second time so they can confirm it.
- Set a personal goal to *speak with* two or three associates a day. Date and jot down the notes and set a follow-up date in your (electronic) calendar. Include your notes in a calendar reminder so you can refer and build on them. Update the notes and move the reminder forward to the next day/time you say you will contact them. Of course, when this day comes, make the call.

- Reach out to folks who know you and know what you can do and how you operate. People you've worked with are THE best people to speak with. Even better than recruiters!
- Use the messaging and recommendation features on LinkedIn to make or renew connections. *Focus on people who know what you can do.*

Wrapping Up the Introduction to the 6-Step Process

You now have a sense of where I'm coming from. I've been in your shoes: unemployed with a lot of financial responsibilities. Having worked with many of people in your situation, I can state categorically, YOU WILL BE FINE! Pace yourself. A Job search is often a marathon and not a sprint.

You should plan to work the **6-Step Process** by getting up at a "business hour" daily. Start with an activity you enjoy. I prefer exercising—walking or running and some push-ups, crunches, and stretching. Swimming is great too. But don't go nuts. A strong body helps keep the mind sharp.

Read a chapter in a book, pray, or work on a project or hobby early before you shower and get dressed for (your job search) work. Dress business casual. Do not stay in your pajamas or wear cut-offs and T-shirts. You want to be ready should you be invited on short notice to a Zoom or Skype discussion. Always be professional. I firmly believe you should maintain a work-like routine during a job search: shower, bathe, and shave daily. You will look more professional and feel better about yourself. This will be reflected in your attitude as you engage with others. It will help you in your networking and job-screen phone calls.

I've heard from several experts who say, "Do not take time off to 'find' yourself." If you wait until your unemployment benefits are expired before you begin and spend your free time vacationing, this may not look good to a potential employer. It could shape their view of you. It might subliminally suggest you are even fine with lazing around. You are not "hungry." Besides, "Daylight is burning!" The process will be long enough. You do not need to extend it by delaying the start. I recommend you work at your job search like a full-time job—because it is! Create a routine that includes breaks and lunch. You do not have to work ten- or twelve-hour days. It is easy to get fried. Plan on a solid four to six hours after your morning (exercise) routine. Create a job search "business day." You can have networking contacts ask you to call them on a specific day and time. Recruiters will schedule screening calls with and for you. Use an electronic calendar that syncs with your phone and use invites. Set reminders. Place emphasis on mental and physical well-being.

Emphasize staying fit and healthy. Working out will help you sleep better too. If you do not pray regularly, now would be a great time to consider religion. Just a thought. You could also consider attending worship services if you do not currently. If you have family or friends that do, consider asking if can join them. Learn. When obstacles (such as job loss) come your way, you realize how good and helpful it is to have a relationship with God. It just is. Finding spiritual peace can make it easier for people to help you.

You will want to be up and operating by 7 or 8 a.m. Around 7:30 a.m. is one of the best times to get people on the phone. I will get into this in more detail later. Working in a vacuum can become unhealthy and unproductive. Blindly applying for jobs online can be discouraging. Investing time without any chance of success is demotivating. Stay upbeat! Applying online can dominate your search time. If not done selectively, however, *you are wasting time*. As mentioned earlier, networking is the number-one thing you can do—let people in you industry know you're a free agent!

Start by setting a goal of speaking with two to three people per day. Sounds easy. You may be asking, "What do I do with the rest of the time?" Well, catching folks at a time when they can speak with you can pose a challenge. You may find it takes a lot longer to actually reach someone on the phone than you may have thought. The networking factor in your search may go on for months, so do not call your entire contact list in week one.

Another good use of your time is to research companies to target. Learn about industry trends. Once you start interviewing, you will be researching the companies and the people you are scheduled to meet. This is preparing for an interview. There is plenty to do, so pace yourself!

Interestingly, you will be doing more research than you might have expected. This is the "new normal" for job searching.

The Yikes! 6-Step Process

Now you can finish your first read of *Yikes!* Or you can take a break here and go for a walk. But, please read through the entire book. There is a flow to the process. If this is your second pass through, you are ready to begin the **6-Step Process**, which falls into these categories:

1. Career and Skills Assessment
2. The Resume
3. LinkedIn and Applying Online
4. Phone Screens and Interviews
5. Negotiating an Offer
6. Networking and Helping Others

I believe you will find a sense of connection with me through the process. I believe in helping others. It is my calling, or one might say, my life's mission. I find it satisfying to help associates, friends, and even total strangers in this intense and sometimes difficult time.

Once you land and are gainfully employed, take a moment and congratulate yourself! Enjoy and celebrate with a friend or family member. I strongly suggest living the final step, "Step 6: Networking and Helping Others." Take some time to call and offer help to others. This will keep your network active and valuable to your colleagues and yourself should you ever need to job search again!

STEP 1

CAREER AND SKILLS ASSESSMENT

This section will help you reflect on your career critically by listing out the interests, experiences, and skills you have accumulated that can be listed on an updated or newly drafted resume.

You should also reflect on your age, interests, wealth, and ability to do something new or different in your career such as moving into consulting, buying a franchise, or changing industries—or maybe even retiring with an emphasis on volunteering.

Career and Skills Assessment

Your job-search journey is best built on a solid foundation—one that begins with an honest, introspective self-assessment. You will want to write down your interests, experiences, skills, and competencies (the tools in your toolbox). You will need to give thought to where you want to go with your career. Do this in the context of understanding why an organization would hire you. John

DiNallo, a longtime industry friend and professional recruiter, advises seekers to "take an inventory of your abilities." What you bring to market is why people will hire you. How you will solve their need or "pain."

Please get used to this notion and internalize it:

> It is not about you but rather about how can you address the needs of the hiring organization—as expressed in the job description.

You will hear me refer to the "requirements as outlined in the job description" or their "pain points" often. Not only do you need to be able to address these criteria but you also need to factor in how they fit with your career plans. Would the position add to your marketable experiences and skills? Ask yourself these two questions: Where do I want to grow? How does the opportunity help me achieve my goals?

However, if you are not genuinely interested or qualified for the position, you are simply "whistling Dixie" by applying for that job. You're wasting your time. The only justification to apply to such an opportunity is if, through your research and networking, you have determined it is a great company with other potential opportunities. Applying to get into a company's line of sight and database is acceptable. More often than not, however, when the fit is not there, you will be better off searching and networking for better opportunities. Do not waste your time applying to ill-matching opportunities. Do not write fiction either in an attempt at consideration.

In this first step of six, you'll want to think about what interests you and if those interests align with your career aspirations. Be critical. In other words, is there a skill or competency gap that contributed to your current situation? Should you take your career in a new direction?

I heard a story regarding a guy (I believe his name was Ron) who was an exceptional chef was an exceptional chef and made good money at it in high school. He chose to keep working and opt out of attending college. After about fifteen years, his interest level and quality of work declined. He lost his passion. Long hours, working holidays, and boredom led to work dissatisfaction. He considered doing something different and assessed his interests and skills. Upon reflection, Ron felt his hobby of painting cars could be rewarding. He enjoyed the accolades and built quite a reputation for his work (his clients told him he had a knack, was way above average, was a real artist, etc.). He thoroughly enjoyed the process, from the prep, sanding, cleaning, and masking off of sections to the paint job and the finish-wet sanding and buffing work. He thought it was time to make a move into that industry. He started asking around and soon secured a job at a custom auto body shop. Ron made the transition after a few months of networking and flourished in the new role!

The Assessment step is the point at which you must analyze the factors that contributed to your need to find something different. Was it due to business economics, or were you not meeting expectations? Are there areas you need to address personally, or is the company/industry struggling? Would you be better served by moving to a new industry? This might be the time to do it. I made the move into sales, and you can make a career move too. Your career and skills assessment work, which we will get into in this section, will help address these questions.

Do your interests align with your career aspirations?

Give some thought to and jot down the following answers in the context of marketplace value. Would someone hire you to do this? Would they pay enough to call it a career move? This is the time to reflect and evaluate how your interests could help you select your next assignment and employer.

- What interests you? What do you do for fun, hobbies, volunteering, etc.? (Note: "Making a lot of money" is not an acceptable answer.)
- Is it fulfilling?
- Are you uniquely good at it? (Above the line? Way above?)
- Has anyone ever paid you for it?
- Is its benefit to you impactful and valuable? Can you define that benefit in the context of numbers and/or dollars?
- Do any of your strengths and interests create market value?

Assess things you know and like and create market value.

There are no wrong answers—only answers that lead to a greater likelihood of success. Dig deep into what you are good at and enjoy. Hobbies. Chores. Things you have tackled while at work or while simply working around the house. What talents do you possess that you feel would generate real, accountable value? If you volunteer, what skills and opportunities have you developed while doing so? Heck, in the film industry, being a "stand-in" for a production company is basically a function of your body type or coloring—therefore, to that employer, your body dimensions and attributes are the "tools." Yes, people get paid for this. Not sure if it is a career, but it is a stepping-stone since it exposes people to key contacts. I love cutting my lawn and often felt if I had to, I could start up a lawn manicuring business. I know people who make a nice living doing so. We will explore your personal interests further in an upcoming assignment, but for now, just start collecting these hobbies and skills in your head. If you get on a roll, write them down.

I suspect you know and will be able to summarize your interests in no time. You may have to give a lot more critical thought as to whether someone would pay you a livable wage to do it. But I still encourage you to jot all your interests down and think about them in a "potential career" context. Hand-crafting furniture may be a wonderful hobby. No doubt you can become an expert. However, is a "sustainable business" possible? Maybe in your market it would be. We address defining your budget in "Step 5: Negotiating an Offer," which will give you deeper perspective into this important factor. There are financial hurdles to consider regarding self-employment.

YiKES! NUGGET

Great Reference Book: *What Color Is Your Parachute?*

A great additional reference book that complements the steps in *Yikes!* and will assist you in taking an inventory and defining your interests is *What Color Is Your Parachute?* by Richard Bolles. His book, which focuses on introspective analysis and taking a self-evaluation of skills, experiences, and interests as they pertain to market value, also provides many detailed aspects of job-search issues. I strongly recommend you refer to it at this stage of your job search. It is a valuable tool, especially if you are considering a career or industry change, and will help you define your skills and competencies. Bolles' book is updated annually and considers markets, technologies, and trends that will open your eyes to the latest careers and job types—many of which are relatively new. No doubt, the "buggy whip" manufacturing folks back in the day had to rethink their career paths with the advent of the horseless carriage! You get the point. Hey, just trying to "whip" up a little interest in your job search here!

Career and Skills Assessment—The Thought Process

For an in-depth career and skills assessment, I suggest you look back and write down what you have done to earn a paycheck. Here, you will capture experiences, responsibilities, and skill-growth gained through learning and overcoming challenges. An important aspect of this exercise is to define the size and scale of your responsibilities. This is best done through tangible data—in other words, with numbers, dollars, and percentages. Ask yourself: Why was someone paying you to do these tasks at the time? What was the *financial impact*?

Give some thought as to what you want to do. Have a discussion with your family. Include some prayerful consideration as to what you want to see happen with your career—and your life! Is there a way to earn income or profit from where your passion and interests lead you? Is there demand in the marketplace—enough for you to create a sustainable income? Will it cover your household budget? This is the time to see if your interests, hobbies, and passions marry up well enough to your professional experiences to determine whether that combination will create enough marketable value to cover all your living expenses—with savings included.

Be critical and honest. If you are five feet, three inches, becoming a center on an NBA team is not going to happen! However, if you are into basketball, enjoy studying the greats, and have a "sixth sense" for the game's strategy and tactics—combined with persuasive communication skills and a passion for motivation—maybe a high school coaching career is possible. Or a job in the athletic department of a college or university.

YiKES! NUGGET

Critically Evaluate Your Fit to the Job Description

An effective job search involves defining, marketing, and aligning your experience, competencies, and skills to the job's "needs." These needs are listed in the job description. The secret to your success will be optimal alignment. Through research and evaluation, you will determine if the fit is there. What does your research about the company, the culture, and why the job is open tell you? Critically compare the requirements against your experiences, skills, interests, and your personality to determine whether that job is a good fit. We get into this in greater depth in "Step 3: LinkedIn and Applying Online," but you need to keep questions in mind as you perform your Career and Skills Assessment.

The Yikes! **6-Step Process** is sequential. Are you truly capable and qualified by the standards set forth by the hiring entity? This is a theme I'll refer to often. You must be critical when evaluating your "fit" to a given opportunity. Even if it sounds like your dream job, forget it if you are not qualified. Unless, through research, you believe the hiring organization is one of your top prospective companies. Only then would I counsel you to invest in applying for or networking into an organization (more on this to follow in "Step 3: LinkedIn and Applying Online").

Interestingly, many jobs that are in development within an organization are *not* posted online—yet. Experience indicates there are numerous situations in which employers know they have a need but have not quantified it. A job description or budget does not exist yet. However, they will act when they find a candidate that they believe—based on their background—can deliver. They will work to fit the right candidate into the company. Getting plugged into such opportunities is a result of networking. Many positive results have been realized by making connections to "hidden opportunities." I can't overstate this enough, there are plenty of opportunities that companies create and fill based on a candidates background, knowledge, and interest.

Your Skills Toolbox

Think about your skills as tools in a toolbox. Scott Boothby, a longtime friend and business associate, has expertise in mergers and acquisition implementation. He uses the toolbox analogy when helping associates impacted by a merger or takeover to see experiences as tools to get work done. A hammer, saw, and screwdriver all have specific purposes. When you see your skills and competencies as tools for a job, you can then see how they can address needs expressed in a job description. Data Analysis, Negotiating, Consultative Selling, Inventory Management, Production Scheduling, Technical Training, and Product Installation are all skills, or "tools." They have market value *and* are transferrable.

So then, which of your "tools" are well-honed, effective, and in-demand? What other skills do you want to develop and add to the toolbox? Does the position you are considering draw on your experiences? Do you have enough to be considered? Could you improve or add another to your toolbox—in a new role?

Would the employer value *paying* you to take courses to get certified? Negotiating for the cost of training or certification would be a good point to bring up to a prospective employer during a phone screen or interview. This can be additional compensation they provide you as we will discuss in "Step 5: Negotiating an Offer." It also sends a great message—that you are dedicated to continual learning.

As stated above, this would be a good time to invest in the book *What Color Is Your Parachute?*. It gives you some self-evaluation, skills inventory assessment, and tools definition questionnaires to use. It is a must for anyone involved in a job search.

Take an Inventory of Your Assets

You have identified your interests and the potential to work with or adjacent to them. Next, you must create a list of your experiences, competencies, and skills (tools)—the top three or four of each. You can rank them in order of importance to your industry or the markets you are researching. These have been uniquely earned and learned by only you. They not only define you but also determine the value you can add to an organization.

Experiences are summarized by the titles you have had. Some examples are:

- Copy Writer & Editor—Pharmaceutical Public Relations
- Paper Mill Production Supervisor | Fourdrinier Wet End
- Sales Representative—Airline Route Optimization Software
- Systems Architect | Commercial Banking
- Design Engineer—Automatic Transmissions | On Highway Truck
- Group Life Insurance Sales—Hospitality Industry
- Product Manager—Software | Education Markets
- Paint Sales & Consulting | Retail

YiKES! ASSIGNMENT 3

List Your Experiences, Competencies, and Skills

List your top four to eight work experiences:

1. _____

2. _____

3. _____

4. _____

5. _____

6. _____

7. _____

8. _____

Competencies are areas of specialization. These represent topics you are experienced in, confident when discussing, and could teach to others. Examples are labor contract negotiating, electrical troubleshooting, residential home design, consultative selling, marketing campaign design, software installation and training, automobile service writing, construction jobsite management, or ready-mix batch plant operations. Working a job at which you attempted to sell cars for four months is not a competency. However, managing an automobile dealership sales team of eighteen sellers for twenty-plus years (Automotive Sales Management) certainly is.

List your top competencies developed over the years (at least four, though you may have several). The ones developed in the last ten to fifteen years will be considered your strongest:

1. _____

2. _____

3. _____

4. _____

5. _____

6. _____

Skills are industry specific areas of specialized expertise, some even certified, that you have learned, tested in, and mastered over multiple assignments. Examples could be certificates earned for intermediate or advanced Microsoft Excel, Word, and/or PowerPoint, certified maintenance vibration tech level I, securities sales (Series 7 brokerage license), physical therapist license, board certified non-destructive test engineer level II, real estate license, X-ray technician, or board certified physical security professional. Negotiation, contract review and writing, and consultative selling are some skills earned over time.

List the top skills you have "mastered" through work or qualified for through certification (two to four):

1. _____

2. _____

3. _____

4. _____

The previous lists are relevant to jobs you are interested in or may be transferrable into a new industry. Write them down and certainly add to them to your developing story. Creating these lists will get your juices flowing. It will offer perspective to your career. For those who have not written or updated a resume in several years, creating these lists will get you in the right frame of mind. You will get into a "groove!" You might even want to post these on your office wall or work area!

YiKES! NUGGET

Keep a Notepad and Pen on Your Nightstand

When you are initially building your career body of work, always keep a pad of paper and a pen handy. I tend to recall critical ideas when trying to fall asleep and find writing them down relaxes me by knowing I have properly captured those thoughts. The process helps me get to sleep. Same for waking up. A pad and pen on the nightstand are a must.

Personally, I carry a small pad and pen with me at all times. I wear oxford shirts with a vest pocket or cargo shorts to carry them. I capture suggestions for books and movies, restaurants, phone numbers, etc., from people I meet. Ideas for business can arrive in an instant—and go just as fast. You can input stuff directly into your phone too. I find jotting stuff down is quick and demonstrates interest. People appreciate it when you take notes—it illustrates attention to detail.

Regarding your job search, the "voice memo" feature in your phone is a good tool too. Just remember to play your thoughts back so you can capture those ideas later. Random thoughts may lead to key ideas that will make your resume stand out.

The Job Search Process: Some Macro-Phenomenon— Part One

Advancing your career to a meaningful state is a "never-ending" progression. For younger folks and/or recent college grads looking to start a career, this fact can be daunting. For those looking to advance a career or those looking to find work after a downsizing or termination, a job search can be humbling yet exhilarating. I know. I've experienced both, and I've met hundreds of people with decades of valuable, successful experience who will tell you they feel uniquely alone. Your specific body of work and your life experiences are what you "bring to market." And eventually, you are either going to get hired "at-will" by way of an "employment contract," as a "1099 contractor" (no benefit access or contribution—a 1099 is used for tax purposes), or by working for yourself. God has equipped you with a one-in-a-million skill set and series of life experiences. They are needed and have market value! No matter what the skill is, you can find people who need and value it. They are there! Understand, however, that the market sets the value. Brain surgeons create more value than, say, bus drivers—but both are in demand and have value. Remember, the world needs ditch diggers too—so take some time to package yourself as a competent one.

For some employers, your value comes in the form of reliability; i.e., you can pass a drug test, have a high school degree or GED, have basic math and writing skills, are willing to learn, are a good team player (learned by playing team sports), are well-groomed (personal appearance, style of dress, etc.), and are in good physical shape! These may be the requirements of someone needed to work in a manufacturing facility, distribution center, restaurant, shipping department, or retail. Regardless, your experiences, competencies, and skills are an entrée into that workplace market. Take pride that you bring a unique "package" to market. You may be surprised to learn that some areas, such as basic reading, writing, and mathematical skills, may be in demand for many positions. That means that growing and sharpening basic skills will increase your market value. You will get paid more because you have them!

College graduates and white-collar professionals have other skills supported by a college degree and, in more recent years, often learn technical competencies as well. Such job-seekers may be competent in Microsoft Office Suite—PowerPoint, Word, and Excel—at beginner, intermediate, or advanced levels. You may also have administrative, people management (hiring and firing), marketing, selling, or other skills and related experiences that only you bring to market. And, of course, the mid-career professional has all these skills, along with a career "body of work" defined by their past and present job titles, assignments, and results. Hopefully, the assessment you have just completed has brought to mind some areas of responsibility, competency, and skill you might not have recognized at first. In some instances, these may have gone dormant. But they do exist and have value. You can never unlearn how to mow a lawn.

Career "Zigzag"

There is another consideration to make. During a downsizing, or if you are a recent college grad who wants to go in a different direction from their degree, consider a move into a new field or industry. In other words, take a career "zigzag." I'll concentrate on mid-career job-seekers here as college graduates have a different challenge. They need to package and sell what they have done in co-ops and summer jobs and learn how to frame these experiences as valuable in the new industry. Youthful exuberance will help!

Back to the mid-career folks. You have been cut loose after ten-, fifteen-, or twenty-plus years and are now looking for work. Depending upon your appetite for change and your financial situation, this may be the time to make a career change. See this as a unique time to go into another industry or into a different type of role. You could move to consulting, to contracting as a 1099 freelance associate, or into another industry or role altogether. These situations have increased risk, but if your spouse has access to healthcare, it may be feasible.

Regarding healthcare, if you need immediate protection for your family, and I suggest we all need at least catastrophic coverage, you should take some time and investigate your options in the Healthcare Marketplace. If terminated with severance your employer may provide coverage for a period of time or let you buy in at the "COBRA" premium levels, but that is expense! If you're under 26 years of age, you can still get coverage under your parents plan if they have one. Medicaid is an option for low-income situations but that may take time to establish, hence you may be better off shopping. The link to the government marketplace in in the appendix or you can search the Affordable Care Act also known as "Obamacare". There is a link to a helpful premium calculator there too. The cost of healthcare needs to be factored into what type of job you seek permanent or part-time given your unique skill set and situation. Maybe you are able to do to more contract "1099" work and need to buy your own insurance – it's off to the market you go!

An example of a career "zigzag" was explained to me by a friend who operates over forty hotels. He told me how tens of thousands of hospitality-industry employees are currently faced with 10 to 25 percent fewer hiring establishments (due to closings) at which to work. Those remaining businesses can now pick from a larger pool of available talent—or excess supply. Many people in hospitality are now moving to the eldercare industry. Both types of industries are similar as they have guests, restaurants, entertainment, and activity centers, but the latter is growing nationwide! This isn't an example of a radical career change, such as going from sales to purchasing; it is a change of market with unique needs. Call it a career "zigzag." Give this some thought. Does a similar opportunity exist for you?

When you are looking to move into a new industry, you will want to strengthen your message regarding your transferable skills such as managing and motivating people, customer service, consultative selling, and problem-solving. Have strong examples practiced and ready to share when asked.

George's Liberation

I have a friend who was dumped five years ahead of his retirement target age; however, he had a savings plan and received a lucrative severance package. He felt liberated. He was not stressed over losing his job due to his financial security. His job had been tolerable, but he certainly did not love it. George saw this circumstance as a relief. He is now considering a new direction that could involve his passion for club sports car racing or real estate—or both.

George had rocketed up in a large organization, gaining more exposure with larger areas of responsibility, and had met all expectations during his career. He is smart, articulate with financial info, and smooth with people. He is presently working on a lake house, preparing it for year-round living. This will create value and give him time to contemplate what he would *like* to do. He will undoubtedly package his experiences and transferable skills and, later, set a new course. I am confident he will succeed. George has taught me critical-thinking skills, exhibited excellent interpersonal technique, and shown me how to work smart and stay focused on the big picture. I'm excited to learn about his next steps and where his career and life will go. I hope you are currently not too stressed about your situation and are ready and able to pursue a job *you* like. There are definitely opportunities out there in which you can turn lemons into lemonade!

We all know folks in jobs trapped by a high-salary lifestyle and who pursue a soulless "things accumulation" existence. I've seen too many people chase the "high" of the latest sportscar, massive boat, or exotic vacation. Those trappings are wonderful but often only offer short-term satisfaction. I learned early in my career that this was not the lifestyle for me. If you have a passion for what you do, it is not burdensome work. For me, problem-solving and selling are fun and stimulating. I enjoy working with people, asking a lot of questions, and communicating with technical people (engineers) to solve problems. I enjoy bridging the various personalities involved, verifying the problem, and solving it. It has been not only rewarding financially but also very satisfying on a psychological level. I think it is why I have pursued helping so many people over the years in their job search and have invested my time in writing *Yikes!*. I'm in my "zone." I hope you find your zone too. Right or wrong, we spend a lot of time at work. It defines who we are and how we live. It is vital to find a work/life balance.

So, take this time to find and explore working where your passion is. If you and your significant other (if applicable) have the risk tolerance and drive to seek the adventure offered by an entirely new gig, go for it! If you can afford to and are comfortable with risk, this period of unemployment you've found yourself in might be the right time to make the move. At least give it some thought. Understand that "no" is an acceptable answer.

Another dear friend of mine, Brian, was recently downsized. He immediately took a new career path. Brian has worked on remodeling his own houses for over twenty-five years. He became known for custom work, including hidden storage areas. Abruptly, he lost his service technician job of twenty-plus years. Fortunately, his wife is employed with healthcare benefits. This provided Brian with an opportunity to start a home remodeling service. Brian did not bat an eye during the process. Now, he is working in areas he is passionate about and skilled in: carpentry, residential electric, and plumbing. Brian is wonderful with people and works on creating designs for kitchens, bathrooms, or whatever is required. Pretty exciting for a sixty-year-old dude!

Most are not able or interested in working for themselves. Therefore, finding your next "at-will" employment opportunity is job one. That is just fine.

There are a couple of people I know who were extremely successful with oil change service centers, toner cartridge distribution and refilling, pack and ship stores, and other franchises. You can certainly do some research on these. If not planning an immediate career move, you can still do some research now to lay the track to franchise ownership as part of a long-term plan. I've included some resources for evaluating buying into a franchise in the Appendix. Of course, you can find more resources online. This is not my area of expertise, so let us get back to marketing you for an "at-will" opportunity—which is:

Your job search is all about selling *you!*

A job search means *selling*. Like it or not, that is the world you enter as soon as you start reviewing listings or writing your resume. In this case, you are selling you. I understand how creepy the idea of "selling" can be to some. Selling has connotations of deceit, which makes it seem unnatural for many people. It is challenging and, in some instances, extremely difficult. That is because, as I like to say, regarding selling, "*You are motivating a person to do something they otherwise would not do!*" One of the goals of this book is to make selling yourself less daunting. We will do this together by identifying and building confidence in representing and discussing your career successes, competencies, and skills in a productive way.

People who sell cars are trying to get you to buy a car on their lot, not the car you necessarily want or need. Conversely, you, in your job search, are trying to convince the hiring personnel to "buy" your unique package of skills and experiences. You do this by matching their needs (as expressed in the job description) to your abilities. You may not be the exact match they are looking for, but who is? The good news is, unlike the car dealer, this is not a high-pressure sale. It is a consultative sale. What you need to do is connect the dots for them, linking your interests, skills, and experiences to the requirements of the job description in a compelling and factual manner.

Throughout your job search, your goal is to motivate the hiring team: the human resource contact(s), the hiring manager, and, often, a senior leader in the company who will ultimately select or "buy" you. Your goal is to convince them you are the best-qualified person to solve the needs as outlined in the job description—easy enough to conceptualize yet challenging to execute. First, you'll need to analyze several factors. How current is the job description? Does the hiring manager today value the same things outlined on the job description posted weeks ago? Are the job circumstance and competitive landscape the same for the company? Your research will help to confirm or cause you to step back and ask more questions when speaking with them.

You will be left at the altar, rest assured, several times or constantly–depending upon how aggressive you are in your search. Get used to it. Job searching is like acting. Collect, appreciate, and learn from rejection (from failed casting calls). Take satisfaction in knowing the more rejections you accumulate, the harder you are working in your job search. You will become a pro at skills matching, phone screening, and interviewing. You learn by doing! More on this in "Step 4: Phone Screens and Interviews." Job search is an iterative, learning experience.

The Job Search Process: Macro-Phenomenon— Part Two

Most of the job-seekers we've worked with at the North Canton Executive Networking Group (NC ENG)—over a thousand and counting from both the job search and recruiting side—agree that job-searching is growing more difficult. There are many reasons and theories why:

- There are more people applying to a given posting (sheer volume).
- More unqualified people apply for jobs or stretch the truth when applying, creating churn.
- HR people struggle when evaluating candidates as there are so many elements the hiring managers expect to be fulfilled.
- Great candidates get disqualified during the courtship due to a negative social media issue, a failed drug screen, or a criminal record.
- Candidates apply for jobs versus thinking about developing their career and quit or get fired soon thereafter as a result.

- Hiring managers are overwhelmed with an increasing crescendo of demands and data to synthesize when evaluating candidates, creating "dithering."
- The costs to terminate associates are increasing, which also delays hiring decisions.

Another aspect of job-search involves employing the mindset that you are always one moment away from pitching yourself. Networking at church, car clubs, the gym, or when shopping or out to eat is commonplace. Therefore, your casual dress needs to be a tick above average. In other words, even when making a shopping run for groceries, I'd suggest you wear a button-down or collared sports shirt versus a T-shirt and dockers or khaki slacks instead of torn-up jeans—unless, of course, you are in the middle of a nasty project and are running to the hardware store. The point is, for most casual outings, think about the potential to make a first impression. Look good and have a crisp "Elevator Speech" ready. Always have your personal "networking" business cards handy (I keep a few *fresh* cards in my wallet). I get annoyed when someone hands me a card that appears to have been in their wallet for years, abraded and worn—not a professional first impression. More on these topics follows in the additional steps included in this book.

Recruiters—You Will Love and Hate Them

With all due respect (and some of these people are my friends), recruiters are often a necessary evil. There are two types: retained and contingency. Retained recruiters rule people out. Contingency types rule people into opportunities. These definitions are courtesy of Mark Morek, a professional recruiter and friend.

When they sense you are a fit, they will become a fast-turned-friendly voice, coach you on how to handle an interview, and share background on the company and people you will meet. Recruiters on a "retainer" (i.e., paid regardless of placements) are employed by client companies. They work in the best interest of their client, the hiring company—not yours. They are paid to scan the market in search of talent for opportunities only the client company has shared with them. These opportunities are not always made public as they do not want to be inundated with low-probability, unscreened candidates. Retained recruiters understand on a strategic level where their client is going, the type of people best suited to the client culture, and the personality traits that succeed long-term with their clients.

Retainer recruiters can be extremely helpful and good to know. However, if you do not show up on a given opportunity, they may quickly drop off your radar—or more likely, they will drop you off theirs. That is because a retained recruiter knows exactly what the client company needs and, more importantly, understands the cultural issues, personalities, and intangibles that lead to a good placement. When they are presenting you, they know very well you are a solid prospect. When the dance is over, and if you are not selected, you will likely never hear back from them. Ever. They will typically advise you that the courtship is over, period.

Contingency recruiters are less connected with hiring companies at the strategic level and use publicly posted openings to attempt to match people to them. In general, all recruiters are paid on a commission schedule. This means the recruiter is not completely reimbursed until the candidate completes a duration of work after placement. The term could be six months or more. Contingency recruiters bring value as they match your skills to openings; however, they are looking to make a (quick) deal, so they are motivated to make a placement. Just like a retainer recruiter, they may not have your best interests at heart. Therefore, they will take less time prepping and coaching you. But they can provide great opportunities in each market and can have good insights into companies they have long-term relationships with.

I recommend that you not pay for recruiting services. It would be unusual for a job-seeker to be exclusively represented by a recruiter or placement firm. Those types of arrangements are too restrictive and are to be avoided.

Getting Left at the Altar—It Happens Often

Opportunities will progress and take on a life of their own. Some opportunities can progress quickly. You will likely experience the infatuation of a quick courtship. However, things can go cold in an instant. Recruiters or HR contacts may just stop following up. Go dark. Ghost you. When this occurs, do not take it personally. They are at the mercy of the hiring manager. The reasons the dialogue may stop can be darn near infinite. They may have filled the role, decided not to fill, or want to continue looking.

The lack of feedback happens all too often and is unprofessional. Recruiters are paid on a commission basis, so letting you down gently is not a priority of theirs. There is little money in it. Yes, that does stink. I'm preparing you as it could happen. Possibly a lot. Do not take it personally. Understand that the recruiter's mission is to find several candidates who meet unique job requirements. They will present numerous candidates in the hopes one will be selected. Recruiters can be a necessary evil. They are aware of positions and may be a gateway to a great job. But they are likely not operating in your best interests. Be polite and, of course, work with them when they call. But do not get too emotionally invested with recruiters. I've stayed in touch with some recruiters for several years. Many are friends. I refer people to them routinely. John DiNallo and Mark Morek gave me valuable industry insights when they reviewed the early manuscript of *Yikes!*.

Career and Skills Assessment—Some Reinforcement

I'm going to reinforce some key elements here. You bring a unique, one-in-a-million set of interests, skills, and experiences to the marketplace! God has not given anyone on the planet the "package" you have assembled. Whether a high school graduate, recent college graduate, mid-career journeyman, or high-flying executive with an Master of Business Administration (MBA), there are no two job-seekers alike.

Job searching requires you to rigorously evaluate what you have accomplished and then to do your level-best at explaining it on your resume. Get good at describing your skills in a quick, concise, thirty-second "Elevator Speech." Said another way, become efficient at telling your story in thirty seconds.

YiKES! NUGGET

Develop a Thirty-Second "Elevator Speech"

Developing a professional, thirty-second Elevator Speech takes thought and practice. I recommend that you do this with another person so you can hear yourself give voice to your story. Should you have the opportunity to join a job-seeker group, even via a Zoom meeting online, be sure to crystalize your message in a nice, tight summary.

First, introduce yourself, clearly state your name, and ask for the name of the person you are speaking with. It is a good idea to repeat their name back to them when you start your speech.

Here is how I characterize my consultative, technical selling career. These would be the elements of a brief explanation to a recruiter, hiring manager, or possibly a stranger who asks, "So, what do you do?" or, "What do you want to do?"

Example Elevator Speech

"Thanks for asking, Fred. My name is Matt Ostrofsky. I'm a professional consultative seller. I sell bearings, belts and chains, and other mechanical products that keep factories running. I solve technical and commercial problems. I work with industrial distributors in both maintenance and repair (MRO) and original equipment (OEM) manufacturers. I'm fortunate to have the opportunity to work with different types of people from the factory floor all the way to the board room. No two days are the same. I work in a broad range of process industries, where products are made. Those industries include food and beverage, construction materials (cement and aggregate), paper making, and steel production. Basically, we ask a lot of direct, open-ended questions to determine the root cause of problems and find solutions. I'm the factory expert who makes my distributors look good. I consider myself a player/coach leading by example to help the distributors learn and grow. Due to a reduction in force, I'm presently a 'free agent' looking to help a new team be successful."

Should you be asked to give your personal briefing, career overview, or "Elevator Speech," in a public setting say your name first, tell your story, and conclude by restating your name. It could happen at a job-seeker group, trade association meeting, or networking event. Let them know you will available during a break or after the meeting to discuss opportunities and network.

Career and Skills Assessment—Summary

Take an inventory to summarize your body of work.

- Reflect on your career and list your:

  - Experiences
  - Competencies
  - Skills

- Points to remember:

  - You could be left at the altar
  - Understand the "One-in-a-Million You"
  - Define your story and write and practice an "Elevator Speech"

You are ready to package your story in a resume. This is real progress! Take a moment to savor these achievements and know you are working the **6-Step Process** and not floundering. Remember: These are living documents, and you will add to and refine them. Your Elevator Speech will improve with practice. And you *will* practice more ... because you care!

Now, let us work on building a great resume together, shall we?

STEP 2

THE RESUME

The resume is a vehicle to capture your career body of work. It connects you to a job opportunity. The better you tailor your background to the job, the greater the chances you will be contacted. There are three basic types for experienced people: Chronological, Functional, and Combination. I recommend a unique "hybrid" layout for recent college graduates.

In some instances, most notably for senior executives, a one-page "Marketing Brief" may be a better representation of a long and diverse career—which offers value in a myriad of areas.

Resume Fundamentals

Writing an outstanding resume is time-consuming and can be especially difficult for a novice. It is a skill to be learned. Certainly, you can pay someone to write it, but customization and "tweaking" can make this approach expensive. It may take too much time as well. Additionally, there is the risk that a professionally written resume, which does not speak the way you do, will raise a red flag to recruiters and hiring personnel.

A resume is a "living document." It is dynamic. And it will improve over time. Your resume needs to be tailored to each opportunity. You typically have only six to twelve seconds to get the reader's attention. Therefore, you should start learning how to write and improve it. Get into the process. If you feel you would benefit from using an expert in the field of resume writing there are writing services listed in the Reference Section.

Organize your work history, listed in chronological order, and include the company name, city, state, and job title with the start and ending duration dates. I'm a big believer in using Microsoft Word for this task. Do not use resume templates. By using paragraphs and bullets, you can build an effective resume quickly. Some of the templates have quirky formatting issues, which make changes difficult for the average novice. Keep it simple. I recommend choosing between the Arial or Calibri (Body) fonts.

A chronological or "traditional" layout works best for most people. Avoid using anything other than text to create the message. No lines, embedded images (i.e., charts), or photos. Companies use Applicant Tracking Software (ATS), which cannot process images and may jumble your experiences on your file. We will get into more details on that later. Additionally, your resume will be viewed on a smartphone, tablet, and/or an iPad, so it is best to keep it fact-based, tight, and efficient.

YiKES! NUGGET

The Four-Part Resume Structure: For the Experienced Professional

As mentioned, you have only about six to twelve seconds to compel the reader into thinking, *I've got to call this person.* You want the reader to read through your resume, then set it aside for further consideration. This implies a quick decision is made; hence, we are all about the facts.

Your resume should be organized and easy to read—no more than two pages long.

Busy fonts, multiple fonts, lines, bars, adding photos or company logos, etc. can all distract the reader. However, some folks who use such complex resume layouts have success. Folks with advertising or marketing communications experience and/or are seeking such industry employment, for example, may use more elaborately designed resumes to showcase their creative skills. This makes sense for opportunities in the arts and/or creative industries – but not for other roles.

For all the experienced folks and professionals out there, however, I recommend this time-tested, and proven-effective layout of a four part chronological resume:

- Professional Summary
- Competencies
- Experience
- Education

YiKES! NUGGET

Include a Compelling Professional Summary

A Professional Summary section should be tailored to address the specific, mission-critical needs expressed in the job description. The top half of page one needs to match you to the job description. Remember: six to twelve seconds. It must have a high keyword match percentage, be compelling, and include a memorable hook or catchphrase that is uniquely you. We will address the keyword match in a bit.

The job search experience is all about finding opportunities with companies you want to join and that offer work you know you will enjoy doing and a culture that has the kind of people you want to be around. However, to land a job and thrive, you must have the skills and experience required. It is up to you to clearly communicate this! Your skills (the tools in your toolbox), interests, and experiences must address the company's needs as expressed in the job description. Doing this better than other applicants will get you noticed. Keep in mind there will be dozens, if not hundreds, of other applicants for that job posting. This is why companies often use software programs with artificial intelligence (AI), known as Applicant Tracking Systems (ATS), to screen out applicants based on whatever keywords/phrases those companies deem necessary to see on a submitted application.

Incomplete, inconsistent, or poorly worded resumes with typographical errors will lead to rejection. If you are not taking the time to correct for grammar and spelling now, companies will assume you will not do so at your work either. Remember, job search is a full-time job, and your professional best is required. There are too many applicants you must compete with, and time is too precious. If writing is not your strong suit, have your work proofread by others – heck, it's good to *always* have someone else review resumes and cover letters before submitting.

YiKES! NUGGET

The Four-Part Resume Structure—College Graduate

For recent college graduates, making the classic transition from high school through university, the top skills you will be marketing are your education and experiences learned while in school. To best showcase those skills, list them using these terms and in this order:

- Education
- Experience

- Skills and Competencies

- Involvement

In this layout, your education is featured, followed by your experience(s) in the field of study or your experience(s) gained through your co-operative work experiences and/or through part-time jobs. Skills and competencies, for example, are considered experience with software programs and other specialty machinery or lab diagnostic or other equipment you can operate. If you've learned how to operate a skid-steer loader (i.e., Bobcat) while working a summer landscape job, add it. This may be unrelated to your long-term career interests, but it shows a willingness to work and improve your knowledge and may help you connect to a hiring manager. You may find your future employer operates a landscape business (on the side) and sees your skill as a potential leverage point. This is true even if you are an accounting and bookkeeping major.

In the Involvement section, list activities such as intramural sports, volunteering (i.e., Habitat for Humanity, soup kitchen, Big Brothers Big Sisters, etc.), and any sorority or fraternity memberships "Greek life." You will find an example of a Recent College Graduate resume in the Reference Section of this book.

YiKES! ASSIGNMENT 4

Start Your Resume with Contact Information

The contact information section should include your name, metropolitan city and state, cell phone, email, and a hyperlink to your LinkedIn profile. Nothing more. Do not include your street address. Just use the major city you live near. You do not want to be stalked or traced to your home address. You do not need people looking at your home or neighborhood online either.

If you live in a rural area, you can describe the location such as Liberal, KS

(West Kansas). Bourbonnais, IL, is located about sixty minutes south of Chicago and might be better described as "Chicagoland South." For some locations, it may just be best to list the city and state and describe your location when asked.

Y̌IKES! NUGGET

Get a Modern Email Address Domain

One issue a mid-career job seeker needs to be mindful of is "telegraphing" your age. Uh, I think I just dated myself with that reference–LOL. There are ways people can easily decipher your age, but you do not have to make it obvious. No need to add the year you graduated high school or college. Speaking of appearing old, or sending a signal you may (metaphorically) be "playing the sixteenth hole of your eighteen-hole career," using a dated email domain, such as America Online (@aol.com), sends up a big "aged" flag. Scrap it immediately for your job search. Get a Google "@gmail.com" or Yahoo "@yahoo.com" account. Consider using one email exclusively for networking and job searching. This would be the same one on your LinkedIn profile, contact cards, resume, etc. Hey, I have an "@sbcglobal.net" address I keep active just to see how long it will be supported. Others such as "@bellsouth.net" should be scrapped too.

On a related note, a professional security consultant advised not to use your first and last name in an email address. Rather, use a nondescript series of numbers and letters. Hackers love finding such nuggets as your name on the internet.

Use a hyperlink to allow a reader to electronically "jump" to your LinkedIn profile from the header. The creation of a hyperlink is a common, yet slick way to enable, in one click, the reader to access your profile. You'll find steps on how to create a hyperlink in the Appendix.

I recommend putting only your name in the Word document "header" section of Word. Located in the "Insert" tab, choose the drop-down menu under "Header," which will open areas at the top and bottom of a document (the header and footer). Select "Edit Header" and then type your name and center it. It is recommended to use your formal first name, middle initial, and last name. Thanks to the wonderful technology Word offers, your name will appear in the exact same spot on the second page of your resume as well. When you're done typing your name, close the Header section by clicking the "X" to the right in "Close Header."

Next, enter your location, cell phone, email, and LinkedIn hyperlink as the first line of text. This will *not* be in the header but will appear directly below it, at the top of the page. In the following example, only Harriet's name is in the header. Her location, cell, email, and hyperlink are the first line of page one. To save space, just type in "LinkedIn Profile" and highlight the text and click "Link" under the "Insert" tab and type in the address to create the hyperlink. The hyperlink takes an online reader directly to your profile:

Harriet R. Stepsons

NYC Westside | cell 999-999-9999 | HRS2343@gmail.com | LinkedIn Profile

The font for your name should be Arial or Calibri (Body) and in size 14 and bold. The balance of the resume should be in the same font but in size 11.

YiKES! NUGGET

Font types and size

Use only Arial or Calibri (body) font for your resume size 11 (your name can be size 14 and bold) and use only one font and be consistent for the resume, cover letters, and your reference list.

The Professional Summary

Below the header, add a Professional Summary banner. When formatted on the resume, based on the margins and font, it should be no more than four lines high. Write a summary that is about fifty to sixty words. This guideline will force you to keep it concise, compelling, and appropriate to the job. Do not use throw-away catchphrases, clichés, empty adjectives, or many non-impactful words. Think of an air traffic controller and how efficiently they must communicate. The Professional Summary must be efficient, be quick-to-process, and connect directly to the employer's needs in the job description. Try to include a hook or memorable catchphrase but nothing more.

The following are examples of Professional Summaries for the opportunity type they are named after. These would be adjusted to align with job description requirements.

Example Professional Summaries

Here is my Professional Summary for my industrial sales career:

An enthusiastic sales leader with +25 years of experience in engineered solutions sold through industrial distributors. A tenacious competitor driven to grow sales and market share. Sells through education, building trust, friendship, and problem-solving. Strives to create accountable value for partners and end-user customers. A sales process "CRM" systems efficiency hawk disciplined in pipeline management.

"Efficiency hawk" is the hook phrase.

Here is my Professional Summary for my job search counselor role:

A passionate, Christian values-based, master motivator in the areas of career, networking, and life advancement. Twenty years of counseling in the job search process with expertise in: resume writing, networking, interview coaching, and job offer negotiating. Assists college graduates, mid-career, and senior C-suite executives. Grateful to serve others in their job search and encourages others to do same.

"Grateful to serve others" is the hook phrase.

Examples of Professional Summaries:

An applications engineer (ME) applying for a sales engineering role:

Intelligent and driven problem solver, expert in active listening. Determines ideal solution for both company and customer. Strives to determine the root cause of technical, operational, and personnel performance issues with a spirit for continuous improvement. A degreed mechanical engineer who enjoys people, solving complex problems, learning new innovating technology, and global travel.

A distributor database and pricing manager seeking similar work:

20+ years of back-office leadership experience in pricing and database optimization. Expert in team and project management. Specialist in reducing cost and cycle time needed to maintain industrial product offering >12M SKUs. Interfaces with leading global manufacturers using large data analysis tools to lower costs and increase accuracy. Has tested and deployed Automated Programmable Interface (API) technology to seamlessly display vendor data on-line.

A mechanical power transmission products seller seeking another industrial sales role—with a distributor:

Professional seller with +25 years of success in the aggregate, power generation, cement, and food processing industries with MRO and OEM applications. Expert in mechanical power transmission products including bearings, fluid power, conveyor belting, and material handling equipment. Deep product, application, and industry knowledge combined with a tenacious yet friendly consultative, problem-solving approach. Creates strong, loyal relationships by addressing customer needs first.

A machine tool industry (i.e., capital equipment) seller seeking a sales position:

Highly skilled automated machining systems sales professional with +10 years of experience designing custom Cap-Ex systems that cost-effectively meet project KPI and ROI payback requirements. Expert in understanding which material removal process will be accurate and reliable and deliver the tolerances and surface finishes required for aerospace, automotive, and complex ultra-precision parts. Familiar with the most advanced materials used today.

An early career employee seeking a manager or sales manager role:

Experienced account executive with five years of success managing individual, small, and mid-size enterprises (SME) and corporate accounts. Retail and wholesale, haulage, construction, and import and export experience. Expert in sales lead generation, prospecting, closing deals, deposit mobilization, and developing new channels. Comfortable with the sales process, relationship building, and retaining loyal and profitable customers.

A non-degreed, senior inside sales associate seeking same:

Professional inside seller expert in relationship building, problem-solving, and up-selling. Provides "service with a smile" employing an empathetic approach customers appreciate. Confident, dependable, experienced, and hard-working with a solid background including inside sales, opportunity management, technical support, and customer service. Skilled analyst in forecasting, quoting, expediting, and order processing.

A Professional Summary for an early career associate seeking a leadership role:

Extremely organized, quick learner, and proficient in Microsoft Office and Google Docs. Flexible, cooperative team player, reliable, detail-oriented, and conscientious with a positive attitude. Known for delegating work equitably, practicing active listening, and using interpersonal and critical-thinking skills to bring order to ambiguity. Expert in keeping teams focused and operating as a cohesive unit.

A senior-level VP Sales & Operations:

Savvy sales and operation professional with a passion for employee and client relationship development in MRO and OEM relationships. Enjoys enterprise management challenges and has generated sales and margin growth. An engineer with an MBA, not adverse to applying "tough love" as warranted to build confident team members. Expert in industry and equipment used in Oil & Gas [Ethanol], Coal & Wind Power, Food & Beverage, General Manufacturing, Paper Making, and Agriculture.

A senior-level VP Sales & Operations seeking new career opportunities:

Sales & Operations executive and team leader who manages with a sense of urgency, confidence, and integrity. Uses a holistic understanding of supply chain systems for a competitive advantage in negotiating systems contracts. Has P&L experience and accountability with a track record of generating shareholder equity growth. Has a boardroom countenance able to create value at the C-suite level.

A late-in-career sales director seeking new opportunity in the electronic access control industry:

Security and Commerce System sales executive with extensive track record of new business development wins, team leadership, and expertise in closing large projects in the higher education industry. Effective at recommending software with web and cloud components integrated with end-devices that deliver identity validation services to mobile apps. Known for collaborative, trusting, and loyal relationships.

An entry-level associate seeking an opportunity to begin a career and not the next job (stocking shelves):

Dependable, detail-oriented, analytical person with experience in industrial and retail organizations. Uses active listening skills and professionalism to solve customer problems. Strives to keep things orderly. An instruction follower and process hawk with a passion for working smart and getting things done right the first time.

YiKES! NUGGET

Always use a keyword match to optimize your resume

To dramatically increase your connection to the job screener(s), whether it's a HR rookie (fresh out of college) or the hiring manager herself, it is critical that you take the time to perform a keyword match. This is where you identify and embed keywords used in the job description, in your resume (and cover letter). This not only connects you to the screener, additionally, the keyword match is a filter that Applicant Tracking Software uses. High matches are passed through while low matches are filtered out – and no human eyeballs will ever see your application! I strongly advise you to make generous use of keywords or key phrases in the Professional Summary, competencies table, and throughout your resume. Jobscan. com is one such tool that you can use to perform the keyword match. In the Appendix, you will find an example of a resume before and after it was written with respect to a job description for a sales position in industrial power transmission. I used www.jobscan.com and did a before and after. After three attempts to revise the summary, the keyword match rate went from 31 percent to 89 percent, or what the website rates as "great." When you begin applying for jobs, you must do a keyword or key phrase match to increase your chances of getting a phone call. This is absolutely critical.

Professional Summary—In Review

As you can see, a customized and creative Professional Summary section is as unique as the person it represents. There are no wrong answers—just better ones. There are an infinite number of descriptive phrases you can use to describe yourself relative to the job you're pursuing.

Better resumes will have the Professional Summary tailored to align with the top three responsibilities and requirements listed in the job description. Make the connection for the reader!

YiKES! NUGGET

How to Treat Acronyms

Managing acronyms is an art. Commonly used acronyms, such as "Return on Investment (ROI)," are ubiquitous in financial documents in most industries. Unique industry "colloquialisms" should be spelled out. For example, in the super-precision bearings industry, "Total Indicator Reading" (TIR) is a commonplace acronym but may not be broadly understood in others. Therefore, it is recommended to spell out the concept, capitalizing the first letter of each word. Then, add the acronym in parentheses. Example: Software as a Service (SaaS).

The Competencies Table

Competencies can best be served up as bullet points in an Excel worksheet and dropped into the resume as formatted text so common scanning software used by companies can read these words. It is suggested that the background and borders be removed. Use the same font as in the resume. I am a fan of Arial. It is easy on the eyes, modern, and appealing. Calibri (Body) is another font to consider. It is more space-efficient, allowing for a slight increase in the word count in the same number of lines. Thus, it saves valuable resume "real estate" with more letters per line. Times New Roman, or fonts that emulate a typewriter, make resumes look old. This could reflect on you.

Listing competencies is a great way to capture your skills and efficiently increase the keyword match percentage (more on this later). Nine competencies in a table is best (three columns of three) and no more than twelve (four columns of three).

They can be descriptive single words, short phrases, or combination of words. More than that can make your resume look busy and overwhelming. Do not embed them as a picture as ATS software cannot read those words and will not perform the keyword match.

Example Competencies Tables—Job Title and Competencies Below

Front Desk Clerk & Night Auditor (Hospitality Industry)

• Dependable	• Problem-Solving Abilities	• Customer Service
• Attention to Detail	• Inventory Management	• Documentation & Reporting
• Housekeeping & Maintenance	• Microsoft Office Suite	• Contract Negotiation

Sales Manager (Industrial Products)

• Consultative Selling	• Negotiation	• Closing Deals
• Time Management	• Developing Sellers	• Managing Sales Budgets
• Quota Attainment	• New Account Development	• Mechanical Drive Design

Corporate Procurement Executive (Fortune 500 Corporate Procurement)

• Procurement, RFx, RFP/RFQ	• Commodity Management	• Spend Analysis
• Supplier Scorecards	• SAP R/3 Purchasing	• SSM, eSourcing, Emptoris
• SAMPro, Siebel	• Oracle, JD Edwards	• Zoho CRM, Avetta
• Managed Inventory (VMI)	• SAP BW, Crystal Reports	• Taulia, Qlikview, Ariba

Inside Sales – Industrial Distribution or Manufacturing

- PT-Place.com
- Price Files
- Expediting

- Relationships
- SAP
- Call Centers

- CRM
- Multitasking
- Logistics

- JIT Programs
- Oracle
- EDI Portals

The sky is the limit with respect to competencies but keep them real and genuine. Be honest with yourself. Do you consider yourself adequate or above average? Could you teach the subject if asked? The competencies should also be applicable to and referenced as necessary requirements ("keywords") in the job description. Swapping in keywords from the job description is a great way to boost your match rate!

YiKES! ASSIGNMENT 5

Add Your Professional Summary and Competencies Table

Draft your four-line, fifty- to sixty-word maximum Professional Summary statement and create a table of nine competencies (three columns of three). Make sure your Professional Summary is no more than four lines high. Make it connect to the job description, descriptive, and compelling. Remember, you have only six to twelve seconds to get a positive reaction from the reader. Motivate them to think "I need to call this person!"

This initial draft will become the basis of your Professional Summary. You will be better off tweaking and customizing it for *each* job you pursue. The basic content will change and evolve over time as you learn the techniques associated with writing a compelling summary.

Additionally, your career experiences will grow. A resume is a "living document," which continuously evolves and improves. Should you be working with

MS Word, avoid using their resume template and formatting software. It becomes a needless burden. Do not waste time formatting. You will be customizing the resume to match specific opportunities and just using bullets in a standard template, possibly with the margins reduced to leave room for more content per page.

Remember, do not embed the competencies table as a picture as the ATS will not be able to read the words.

The Experience Section

The Experience section lists your work experience by employer and role in chronological order. The most recent is listed first. As you fill in your responsibilities and experiences, you will need to create bullet points that describe what you did and the (financial) impact made. How did you contribute to the enterprise? Why were you paid? Typically, you will have a few more bullet points attached to your recent assignments. These should clearly resonate with the reader and show you are qualified for the job.

Impact!

You must describe the impact of your work—this is the most critical aspect of capturing your experience. Quantify it with numbers, dollars ($), and percentages (%). Describe the impact you've made in each assignment makes for a great resume. "Impact" is the quantified results of your work described with numbers and measured in dollars with percentages. Simply put, as Mark Morek, a principal at Ciresi & Morek says, "You are either making money or saving money for the company—cite examples."

Quantitative examples should be defined with numbers, dollars, and percentages wherever possible. Qualitative results are described directionally with words such as "improved," "enhanced," or "upgraded" or "decreased," "reduced," or "economized."

YiKES! NUGGET

Use Numbers, Dollars, and Percentages to Define Your Impact

Strive to use numbers, dollars ($), and percentages (%) to describe the size and scale of your work and successes. Ironically, most people do not. Doing so gives the reader scale and better describes your responsibilities. By quantifying your results, you increase the depth of your message, creating perspective. The reader is better able to understand how you can impact their role. They can begin to envision you in that job. This gives you a competitive advantage over other applicants.

Examples of typical resume bullets versus better ones:

Typical resume bullet:

- Managed a service center responsible for the Lufkin Texas market

Made better:

- Managed a 12-person sales center generating $25.6M in revenue (with 12% operating income) servicing Lufkin and the East Texas industrial markets

Typical resume bullet:

- Sold perfume in the health & beauty department

Made better:

- Health & Beauty consultant serving twenty to thirty clients per four-hour shift generating average sales of >$600 per hour

It is not necessary to pack each bullet with head-spinning information, but using numbers creates perspective. Your responsibilities and achievements, no matter how large or small, become meaningful. Defining them will separate you from the pack!

Some examples where you can create impact are: the number of people managed, budget value, program, project revenue you (or your team) supported, or dollars sold in a territory.

Most people do not provide impactful data. It is unfortunate. I've scanned hundreds of resumes, and I'm always surprised at how few people know the size and scale of what they do. Probably 85 percent do not include any "dollarized" value of their assignments—thus, no impact is defined. No value they've created for their employers is defined. These employees have been toiling away, making money for their employers with no knowledge or understanding of their impact – their value to the enterprise. Amazingly, this is true for entry-level, mid-career, and senior-level executives. I see it all the time!

When you think about it, anything you are being paid to do will have financial impact on the business. Otherwise, no one would pay you (and provide access to benefits) to do it. This is true for president-level, corporate C-suite executives, D-level directors, managers, and individual contributors. Heck, this applies to forklift drivers! Because so few applicants have this type of data captured in their resume, you can use it to make your resume instantly powerful.

Remember, you have six to twelve seconds to demonstrate your impact and market value. When written with an eye to keywords and impact, your resume becomes compelling. You're more likely to get the desired reaction: a phone call.

YiKES! NUGGET

Resume Guidelines, Dos, and Don'ts

- Do not use the word "I"—never speak in first person on LinkedIn either.

- Do not use contractions.

- Do not embed a photograph (in a resume) as they'll see find your smiling face on LinkedIn once they click on the hyperlink in your contact information.

- Do not embed pdf images, pdf graphs, or charts as they cannot be read by Applicant Tracking Software (ATS). Use numbers, dollars, and percentages to demonstrate impact.

- Do not use an "Objective Statement"—they are out!

  Defining what you are looking for (i.e., your "Objective") and what you want to do is out. Your job search is not about you but rather *how you fulfill the company's job requirements*. Your mission is to find a good fit based on what you are competent at, create value, and will help you progress along your career path.

- Do use a Professional Summary that captures the essence of your career and, when used in a job application, connects you to the job.

- Do match your body of work to the hiring manager's needs.

  It is all about addressing their pain, their needs, and how you can satisfy them better than any other candidate!

  The top half of page one must be compelling—motivate the reader to call you.

- Do quantify your impact by using numbers, dollars ($), and percentages (%) to define the size and scale of your responsibilities and achievements.

  Qualitative phrases such as "increased sales," "reduced scrap," "increased speed to market" are acceptable, but using numbers, dollars, and percentages is better.

- Do not include the phrase "References Available Upon Request." It is a waste of valuable "resume real estate". They will know when to ask you—and at that point, your list will be ready.

SOME TIPS ON CREATING IMPACT

SOAR Stories

SOAR stories are **S**ituations you were in, **O**bservations you or your team made, **A**ctions you initiated or were part of, and the **R**esults you or your team achieved quantified with numbers, dollars, and percentages. These do not have to be multi-million-dollar stories. The fact that you think this way and express the impact of your work in numbers, dollars, and percentages is the key.

Using a SOAR story or two will give you a competitive advantage—and there is fierce competition out there! I will reinforce the need for one or two well-developed SOAR stories in "Step 4: Phone Screens and Interviews." If some situations come to mind now, take a moment and jot down some of the details. An upcoming Yikes! Assignment will help you with this step.

An example SOAR story

For quite some time, my company had been processing distributor rebate claims manually and spending an increasing number of man-hours doing so. We hired a small army of clerks in the "back office" to process these increasingly frequent claims. Rebates were getting mailed in, hand-written on notepads, napkins—you name it. We had no ability to validate the claim accurately or quickly. The growing clerical staff was starting to transcribe these into Excel, so we could process the sheer volume in a traceable, orderly manner. At this point, we realized this process should be automated.

We implemented a software-based, claim-matching system born from a desktop software platform. Distributors would email us the completed Excel spreadsheet to our template requirements, and we would then automatically match on key elements. When the matching was satisfied, the claim would be acknowledged, and confirmation to accounts receivable would then be generated. We could then reconcile invoices based on confirmed, approved claims.

It worked remarkably well. Further, as part of our distributor policy, we required that claims be submitted electronically. An Excel file was submitted to our claims group (attached to an email). This allowed us to reduce the clerical team and eliminated two full-time employees ($65K each, fully burdened), saving $130K annually. A derivative of the system is still in use today!

YiKES! ASSIGNMENT 6

Develop a SOAR Story

You should have a well-developed SOAR story or two defined and practiced. Remember, these do not have to be multimillion-dollar events. Follow the four-part "SOAR" structure, get comfortable telling them, and use them when appropriate. Briefly summarizing them on the resume opens the door to discussing them during a phone screen or interview.

Return on Investment (ROI) and How to Use it Show Impact

- To express impact is critical. This can be expressed as a Return on Investment (ROI). Doing so defines what the company was looking to improve, what they invested in to solve a problem, and the financial payback, or return, that was realized in a specific timeframe. This is an example of a basic return on investment analysis:
- Warranty Claims were ~$750K per year traced to the assembly department

- Commissioned a cross-functional team to investigate the nature of the warranty claims
- Determined employees needed training to eliminate the root cause of the major claim problem: not tightening bolts consistently (not using a torque wrench)
- Formed a four-person team that created training in the corrective action
- It took three months to identify and create the program with these costs:
  - salary $100K ($25K each associate)
  - training materials, tools, and fixtures of $150K
  - investment in year one was $250K
- Therefore, $750K in claims was reduced by investing $250K in year one
  - $750K/$250K = 3 or a 300% ROI
  - This could be savings realized in subsequent years too
  - IMPACT DEFINED!

Please see "How to Create a Basic Return on Investment (ROI)" in the Reference Section.

YiKES! NUGGET

Proper Formatting of Job Duration

How your employment duration is formatted is important. You want the ATS software to easily understand and parse your information. I have learned the preferred format is the two-digit month and four-digit year, separated by either a dash ("-") or forward slash ("/"), then by the word "to." Use the word "Present" if you are still employed in the role. Examples:

Compton Screw Machine Company—Compton, CA

Inspector—Precision Machining Department   **06/2012 to Present**

ABC Company—Garden Grove, CA

Shift Supervisor—Finish Inspection and   **11-2005 to 06-2012**
Pack Department

A Counterpoint on Duration Formatting

If you have a series of jobs with a year or less in service, or you have some gaps, you can consider using only the year (i.e., 2012). In other words, if you had two jobs in the same year, you could use just the years for the entire resume. Example:

ABC Company—Garden Grove, CA
Shift Supervisor—Finish Inspection and Pack Department   **2020 to Present**

Compton Screw Machine Company—Compton, CA
Inspector—Precision Machining Department   **2020**

Cooks Custom Machining—Alhambra, CA
Supervisor—Final Inspection Department   **2018 to 2019**

JCI—Los Angeles, CA
Shift Supervisor—Foundry Operations   **2012 to 2018**

The "12-2006 to 08-2011" format is preferred. Frankly, if not cynically, I think hiring companies prefer this format to readily identify employment gaps and/or age. Your prior experience and dates will be validated during a background check, so be honest. Include all assignments regardless of how brief the duration. But note, the last 10 to 15 years of your career is most important. If your career is extremely choppy, a marketing brief may be required. More to follow on marketing briefs shortly.

Back to the Realities of Job Searching and the Resume

Resumes are now viewed (actually, more like quickly scanned) on a computer, iPad, tablet, or often a smartphone. Therefore, a resume must be easy to read. It cannot be loaded with throw-away catchphrases and clichés. Nor should it be verbose or wordy. You are striving for impactful, concise, and efficient messaging. The words you choose are critical and should be descriptive. Avoid using big words if commonly used—and well-understood—words will do the job.

Always take the time to have a keyword match performed (explained earlier). A high percentage of keywords dramatically increases the chance a real human will read your resume when submitted online:

- Keywords are mission-critical words used to describe what skills, experiences, and attributes the employer wants the candidate to possess – and as listed in the job description. These are descriptive words they know will ensure success.

- The keyword match percentage refers to the identification and comparison of how many of the keywords are in both the job description and your resume.

- You can use the website jobscan.com to create an analysis of the keywords in the job description compared to a resume. It and other websites can identify keywords, list them, and calculate the percentage in both the job description and your resume—the "match".

- Web services such as jobscan.com create a report unique to your resume and one job description. Once you perform the analysis, you can then take the keywords and appropriately work them into your resume prior to applying online.

- Should you apply online (blindly—when no one in the company has asked you to or is aware you are), you drastically lower your odds of getting a call if you do not perform a keyword match. Frankly, you should not even waste time applying online without a doing a match.

One More Thing on Keywords

If your attempts at adding keywords have not been going well, and you are genuinely struggling to work them into your resume, re-think if this is really a good opportunity. Be candid and critical. Just say no. Do not waste your time!

Your time is better spent searching out better opportunities aligned with your career objective and skill set. You would be better off calling someone in your network to check in and say hello. Or call a new person and let them know you are a "free agent" rather than taking the time to apply to a job with a bad fit. You will not get selected. Based on pure statistics, you will be rejected a lot more than selected, so why waste time creating a rejection? Low keyword-match candidate applications rarely get to human eyeballs.

Frankly, you are better off researching opportunities, the company, the industry, the hiring manager, the competition, etc. than blindly applying for jobs online. Do not take long shots. I became good at getting jobs, but I could have done better researching the company culture, personnel, and technologies to help ensure success. Please learn from this.

When to Use a Marketing Brief

What about when someone wants to pass on your resume within a target company but possibly in a different industry...with no specific job in mind? In such a situation, you would be better served by using a marketing brief over a "generic" resume. These documents are not a chronological listing of your assignments but rather a "brief" lists the Responsibilities, competencies, and Successes accumulated in a homogenized one-page document. The brief is helpful when crossing into a different industry, considering consulting roles, or hiding age. It is something to consider for long-tenured, senior executives with a diverse skill set. Examples of marketing briefs are included in the Reference Section.

Resume Structure for College Graduates/New or Returning-to-the-Workforce Candidates

For college graduates, your resume will emphasize your education and any skills developed while in school or during an internship. If you are a parent or student contemplating a higher education curriculum, please seek out programs with a strong internship program. Those experiences and connections are extremely valuable. An example of such a Summary (listed as a sentence or two below your contact info) could be something similar to the following:

Recent graduate pursuing a career in marketing analytics. Has broad experience with analytical tools where advanced skills were attained in Excel and Python. Driven by a passion for accuracy, data clarification, data-driven decisions, and team collaboration.

YiKES! NUGGET

College Internships Are a Great Career and Networking Launching Pad

For future college students and parents, I cannot overstate the importance of selecting a college or university with a well-developed Internship Program. Some call these Co-op Programs. Regardless of the industry or career aspirations a student has, these work-study programs allow the student to gain precious real-world experience. Even more importantly, it begins their professional network with valuable industry contacts. These people may stay in their network (possibly) for their entire career!

Many companies hire college students in specific fields of study. This allows the company to build a relationship while evaluating the student for future consideration. Try finding internships your freshman year—you will want to start networking and asking around during the fall before Thanksgiving break as these jobs get filled in the spring. Apprenticeships are required for skill trades curriculum, so they are a given. Treat internships with a similar mindset—they are a must-have.

I got lucky. My summer work as a mechanic positioned me with a company that hired me upon graduation. They knew me and my work ethic. They knew how dedicated, personable, and knowledgeable of the people and plant operations I was. They trusted me.

YiKES! NUGGET

No Typographical or Grammatical Errors Allowed

Every correspondence you send to a prospective employer, networking contact, or volunteer helping you in your job search should have no typographical or grammatical errors. Use the "Review" tab and then select the "Check Document" feature in Word.

Critical warning here. I have no idea why this happens, but in some instances, the titles (i.e., Professional Summary, Competencies, etc.) are overlooked by the autocorrect in Word! I've seen this too many times and would be remiss if I did not warn you. Check the spelling of the title sections separately. It is an odd issue, but remember, a "typo" is a potential trigger for rejection (remember the aforementioned "filter setting"). It is bad form in a resume or in your work.

Sometimes it is a good idea to read your resume backward—from end to beginning. Read each sentence backward. This old trick can help you "see" errors since instead of reading and focusing on the context, you are scanning for oddities, mistakes, and errors.

Simple, standard formatting is best. When adding an assignment, briefly describe the company to give some perspective. Format the duration of the various assignments with a two-digit month and four-digit year. This is not mandatory but is helpful to the reader. Example:

ABC Corporation
A $5.5B global producer of elastomeric roof membrane systems and install services (NYSE: ABC)
Vice President—Manufacturing   **04-2003 to 06-2012**

Since most sophisticated HR departments will use applicant tracking software (ATS) to select prospective candidates, many factors, including your years of service in each assignment, will be synthesized with this software. "Play nice" with these systems or with the humans who scan hundreds of resumes.

Here are some format recommendations to consider as you list your assignments. Have the company name on one line. Next, include a brief—one line if possible—description. Include the ticker symbol and platform if publicly traded (i.e., NASDAQ: KLMT) but not widely known. List the job title, city, state, and duration (start and end dates, month, and year) on the next line.

Next, you can add a brief description (one sentence or two) to define the essence of the work. Or you can go directly into a bullet list of the most important aspects of your responsibilities. Create perspective and impact by using numbers, dollars, and percentages where possible. Be honest and conservative with these details. If you do not know the details, please do not "wing it." Later, when asked to expand upon this information during an interview, you will feel uneasy, and the discussion will come off as awkward. You can be directionally accurate if you do use estimates. Numbers, dollars, and percentages are extremely helpful to the people evaluating your work for the first time. It gives them perspective. Some examples later follow.

The preferred formats are best described by the following examples:

Below is an example of a resume with no company definition needed for the job-seeker's present job as Hilton Properties is a well-known global brand, but describing the site creates perspective:

Hilton Garden Inn, Sunny Park, MT   **11-2019 to present**

A 620-room ski resort and spa specializing in retired couples and corporate outings

Night Auditor/Front Desk Agent

- Responsible and trusted to balance the revenue and cash transactions at an average $15,000 per day
- Maintains overall operations and appearance of the front desk, providing service with a cheerful countenance
- Interacts with ~75 to 200 guests per day to enhance the customer service experience and create positive perceptions
- Makes reservations, reserves meeting rooms, and addresses special room service requests ensuring a satisfactory guest outcome

A format with a brief company description to define size and scale:

Krell Pumps & Compressors—Hartford, VT   **10-2015 to 12-2018**

50-year-old family-held $30M Northeast distributor of pump & air compressors, parts, and services

Procurement Agent

- Urgently addressed ~2,000 pre-sale customer quotes; maintained log in SAMPro, totaling $48M in potential opportunities, resulting in $3M year-over-year revenue for 3 consecutive years.
- 480 customers, majority of repeat wins were from existing clients with more than 80 suppliers.
- Logged new call-in leads in Zoho CRM supporting 9 outside sellers, simultaneously managed customer RFQs, bid proposals, pricing requests, checking availability, inventory utilization, technical specifications, drawings, and supplying any substantiating information to drive the sale of new complete machines, in addition to setting up new customers with a line of credit.
- Entered and expedited >1,100 POs, with post-sale work orders annually. Coordinated with suppliers and addressed logistics as needed. Processed accounts payable invoicing to close out work orders to maximize overall month-to-month cash flow.

Other examples:

ABC Gear Service	**06-2016 to 06-2018**

Private-equity-held $40M OEM, 125 associate custom irrigation pump design, build, and maintenance services company

Product Development Engineer

Johnstown, PA

- Developed and executed the repair of 12+ new gearbox model repairs after analyzing cost feasibility of proposed industrial gearboxes; contributed to $280K in new annual revenue.
- Sourced components removed from unit during disassembly while gaining minimum of 3 vendor quotes for varying components on a quick turnaround basis.
- Created assembly procedures and document parts with their specifications for reordering and reassembly of new gearboxes within the facility, eliminating eight production days while improving cash flow – a company objective.
- Improved current systems through process mapping and provided suggestions for cost and time savings; goal was to save $30K every quarter, which was realized after three quarters.
- Provided technical training on gearbox operation, oil analysis, vibration testing, etc.
- Maintained four critical-to-quality (CTQ) metrics on root cause of warranty claims; communicated with technicians and office personnel managing timeline and customer service expectations.

The Cross Company—Oshkosh, WI   **12-2002 to 12-2009**

Senior Technical Support Representative (Reno NV)

- Provided technical support to ~500 customers nationwide for bearings and related products valued at $1.2M/year.
- Trained in-person, or via WebEx, new and existing associates in company products and systems; held several one-hour sessions, for 16 to 24 associates per month.
- Responsible for ~75 Western region accounts generating $55M in sales per year with responsibility for order board review, expedites, and quote follow-up and conversion to orders.
- Tracked, measured and reported key performance indicators (KPIs) for analysis including: phone and e-mail response-time, quotation conversion rates, order management and returns, expedites, all types of technical support requested and provided (by product group), assistance with catalog information websites, and other order management systems.

Grady Corporation—Birmingham, AL

Privately held, three-store, 38-person distributor of factory lubrication systems

Seal and Single-Point Lubricator Sales
Specialist—Southeast Region   **11-2015 to 08-2020**

- Promoted to Product Specialist supporting a $2.6M business plan in the 15-person SE Region
- Services 400 distributors, making ~ 325 branch or joint visits annually in a 13-state territory (14 overnights/month)
- Achieved territory goals for sales growth (3.5%) and calls (300+)
- Major end-users include Georgia Pacific, US Steel, Tyson Foods, JBS Beef Pilgrim's Pride
- Won new business worth $130K in 2018 and $158K in 2019
- Trained new employees and distributors; held ~150 sessions/year (6 attendees per)
- Established a $1.9M business plan for SE Region and exceeded goal by 30% in 3 out of 5 years
- Provided sales support to OEM accounts securing large orders; $18K in 2017, $58K in 2018, and $106K in 2019

YiKES! NUGGET

Describe Currency Consistently

Make sure you are consistent when describing currency. Use "K" for thousands, "M" for millions, and "B" for billions with a currency symbol (i.e., US dollar with $). Hence, $134K or $5.7M is fine. No need to slice the numbers finer or to spell out thousands or millions; for example, $2,855,100, or $2.9 million, as it wastes valuable character space or "resume real estate"—use $2.9M. Note, if you are building off of an older resume, please go back through it with a critical eye to make sure you are consistent and uniform. Be professional with every data point on your resume.

YiKES! ASSIGNMENT 7

Add Your Experience Section

Add your chronological sequence of assignments. Can you complete it and keep the resume two pages with room for the Education section last? You should "wordsmith" the document and focus on optimizing for impact.

The Education Section

The final section is Education. In this section, you can title it EDUCATION or EDUCATION & CERTIFICATIONS when you have applicable trade association, software, training, community college, or technical vocational school certifications in your arsenal. Related to education, for the college graduates, is to go back to your institution's Career Placement or Career Development Department for career development assistance. Many of these departments work with alumni for their *entire* careers! Yes, those folks who helped you format your first resume are available to help mid-career seekers too!

You typically will list education last. An early-career, mid-career, or veteran senior-level executive will be hired based on who you know or what you have accomplished. Your 3.8 GPA you earned as undergraduate 20 years ago, will not have as much impact as your career successes. That reminds me, do not include the year you graduated unless you are a recent college graduate. What is critical is that you meet the educational requirements listed in the job description. If you do, you will be fine.

There are two exceptions to this rule: when someone gives you a personal reference or if you have a deep understanding of the role and have had a long career in the industry/role—say, ten-plus years. In this case, the hiring team will consider you based on the personal referral and extensive experience versus meeting the education requirement.

Education section, example formats:

Mid-career industrial sales manager
- The Ohio State University, Columbus, OH
  - BS Mechanical Engineering
  - Business Management Minor
- Software Programs—Microsoft Windows, Microsoft Office Word, Excel, and PowerPoint
- SAP Xsell CRM Software
  - Proficient in SAP ERP system
- Toastmasters
  - Canton, OH Chapter
- Harvard Business Publishing
  - "Managing for Success" Certificate
- Six Sigma yellow-belt training
  - Project: Reducing Scrap Through Better Inspection Techniques

Early career HR professional
- Oklahoma State University, Stillwater, OK
  - Bachelor of Science in H&R Management

Soon-to-be college graduate
- **Materials Science Undergraduate**, GPA: 3.017 | The Ohio State University | Columbus, OH
- Anticipated Graduation: May 2020

Senior-Level Pharmaceutical Marketing Manager
- B.S. Chemistry, Carnegie-Mellon University, Pittsburgh
- MBA, Finance & Strategic Planning, Katz School of Business, University of Pittsburgh

YiKES! ASSIGNMENT 8

Add Your Education Section

The Education section is the caboose on your resume freight train of information! Caboose? The railroads eliminated cabooses in the 1980s. Yikes! Dating myself again!

Your Draft Resume

Your resume is vital to your job search. So, congratulations on creating that draft! Solid resume writing skills are up there with interviewing skills when it comes to what is most mission-critical for success. Remember, the resume generates the phone call. The call leads to the interview. The interview gets the offer. And everything is negotiable. Your resume must be compelling, well-written, and organized. It must not have any typos. And don't forget to take the time to align it to a specific opportunity with a keyword match.

Although writing an outstanding resume is time-consuming and initially difficult, it is a skill that can be learned over time. A life-changing career event, such as a downsizing, requires focus. One area to focus upon is receiving positive feedback on your resume.

Capture your career highlights as they occur. Maintain a resume. There are advantages to doing this during your career, such as:

- Your resume writing skills will improve over time as you practice, rewrite, and update sections.
- You will be better able to recount the successes when you capture and articulate them yourself.
- Keep your resume two pages long—college grads and early career people should keep it to one page.

- You will be able to recall the details (of your "SOAR" stories) with more clarity from writing and developing them.
- Capturing wins as they occur with numbers, dollars, and percentages is easier to do as they happen during your career – so capture them as they occur.
- Annually updating your resume is a great habit. Add a calendar reminder to do so one week before your annual performance review.

This will enable you to react quickly as opportunities present themselves as your career progresses. Instead of writing a resume, you will only need to tweak it to align with the job description!

It is never too late to start. But recognize if you need help. You can always have your resume professionally written if it is beyond your capabilities. Some writing services are listed in the Reference Section.

However, even if you use a service, they will need the chronological list of your assignments, and you will need to provide the responsibilities you were given defined preferably with numbers, dollars, and percentages. You should give some thought to a Professional Summary that captures the essence of you and your body of work. Therefore, since you will need this basic info regardless, start drafting your story right away.

Resumes can take many forms. Be careful not to use a design that is too busy. Colorful backgrounds, photos, and company logos can create the appearance of an advertisement. This "busy" format works for some. However, the content must be industry-appropriate, supported with numbers, dollars, and percentages. Must have plenty of impactful content. It cannot only be "pretty." There is only one chance to make a positive first impression when someone invests the time to read your resume. Make sure your resume is fact-based and well-written, with no typographical or grammatical errors, and has a consistent font. Make it compelling and connected to the specific job for which you are applying.

There are several examples of bad and good resumes in the Appendix section for you to review and follow—or not follow!—when creating your resume.

Congratulations! You've reached a very important step in the process. You have created your draft resume! Savor the moment!

RELATED JOB SEARCH DOCUMENTS

Cover Letters

There is an ongoing debate about the importance of cover letters. Many consider them out and use them rarely, if ever. Others strongly advocate for them. I'm of the opinion that if asked, create one. Make it very good. If you are applying online and the company requests it, provide it. The preferred format is the "T" letter.

The "T" letter structure is simple, clean, and to the point. It clearly connects you by describing how you have the experiences and education required as listed in the job description (and this never gets old) because if you do not, why are you wasting everyone's time?

I recommend to always use a subject line. Add the title of the position with a number (if they reference one in the posting). Have an opening sentence to confirm the position you are applying for and why. List the top four to six requirements in one column. Then list your qualifications in second side-by-side column. Describe how you are a qualified candidate by making it easy for them to see how your experiences meet their requirements.

Example "T" Cover Letter:

ABC Company

100 Main St.

Avon, CT 06001

Subject: Controller—Buffalo, NY (Posting # 10-143A)

Dear Representative:

Please consider my +12 years as Controller in a heat-treating oriented manufacturer and strong interest in joining The ABC Company. I have reviewed your position requirements and believe my experiences and education are a strong fit for the position:

10 years of experience	– Controller at Funk Engineering +12 years
Excel, dBase & SAP	– Advanced Excel & dBase with 4 years SAP

Heat-treating processes	– 6 years of nitriding, gas quench & other techniques
Graduate-level accounting	– Master's in accounting: UConn (3.28 GPA)

I look forward to discussing how my background and experiences align with the position requirements outlined to in the Controller position. Please find my resume enclosed. I look forward to taking next steps.

Sincerely yours,

Joseph H. Wander

A "T" cover letter helps the reader clearly understand you are a strong candidate in a matter of seconds. They can confidently recommend you to the hiring manager.

Personal Business Cards

Once unemployed, you will have hundreds of opportunities to connect with people. You will want to have your contact information on a business card. Some folks suggest you limit it to just your contact information. No need to list your home address, especially if you are part of a family with children or a single female – don't invite stalkers.

As discussed in the contact info section of the resume, you do not need people using Google Earth to search your address and see what type of house or neighborhood in which you live. In addition to your contact info, you can list memorable data such as a high-level description of what you do, valuable certifications, and valuable competencies. But these must be high-level and not box you into one area—unless you want to stay in this field. I've had some folks recommend that you leave any industry stuff off, but I prefer something memorable.

A QR code to your LinkedIn profile (on the back) is becoming more common. But leave some white space on the back blank with a non-glossy finish so there is room should you need to make a quick note.

There are some low-cost, high-quality business card sources you can find online. We list a few in the Reference Section.

The card layout for a plant manager could look something like:

Harold Stickley, Jr.   Chicago IL

Manufacturing Plant Leadership 15+ Years
- Black Belt Lean Expert
- ISO 9002 Compliance Expert
- PETE Injection and Blow Molding

Cell +1 999-999-9999   HaroldSJR@gmail.com

An example marketing director card:

Mary L. Wembley   New York City
Marketing Director—Pharmaceuticals
- FDA Compliance New Product Launch
- Doctor-Patient Relationship
- Big Data Analysis
- Launched Nervexus®

Cell +1 999-999-9999   MLW2001@gmail.com

Adding a QR to your LinkedIn profile is highly recommended.

YiKES! NUGGET

Create and order personal business cards - now!

YiKES! NUGGET

Create Your Cell Phone vCard

Another professional way to make your contact information available is known as a vCard (virtual card). It offers your contact info without your home street address. You need only include the metropolitan city and state. This is a quick way to share your contact info with another phone or via email.

You can select vCard and the "Share Contact" feature on smartphones when viewing your card in "Contacts." Your contact vCard can then be sent via text message or "Air Drop" between two Apple iPhones—if the feature is activated in both. Once the vCard arrives in the recipient's phone, all they need to do is click on the attachment and then "create new contact" and save. The contact info is saved as you sent it—no retyping of data required.

You can also attach a vCard in your email by selecting it from your "Contacts" list. This eliminates typographical errors. It is very helpful and much appreciated, especially if the recipient is unable to write or type—potentially while they are driving. This is a great tool surprisingly few people use. I consider it a professional courtesy in a job search. It just makes it easy for people to help you.

References List

When you begin thinking through your search, secure three or four professional and one or two personal references early in the search process. It is imperative you contact these people and get their approval beforehand. You will want to have your references lined up and ready before you start searching. This will be good for networking discussions as well.

YiKES! NUGGET

Create and Manage Your Reference List

When asked for your Reference List, make sure you alert the people listed as references of a potential call. It is wise to ask them to please reinforce some aspects of your character, skill set, or career successes applicable to the opportunity they will be contacted about. Your references can help you with a mere mention of a competency critical to the role. Better references are typically long-term friends and associates who will describe your strengths. They know you and what you can do!

The Reference List is one page long and organized as follows in this sample:

JOSEPH O'MALLEY—REFERENCES

PROFESSIONAL

Relationship to Joseph—Line manager whom I reported to (known for 12 years)

Susan Rothenberg—Managing Director

ABC Manufacturing, Claremont, CA (Western Time Zone)

Mobile 999-999-9999

Relationship to Joseph—Teammate who worked on same regional team (8 years)

Fred Jones—Regional Manager

ABC Manufacturing, Claremont, CA (Western Time Zone)

Mobile 999-999-9999

Relationship to Joseph—Coworker who reported to me "Direct Report" (7 years)

Gary Woods—Territory Sales Representative

Clark Mining Supplies, Tucson, AZ (Mountain Time Zone)

Mobile 999-999-9999

PERSONAL

Relationship—YMCA Member (12 years)

Roger Harrison

Firefighter—City of Milford, CA

Mobile 999-999-9999

Relationship—Next Door Neighbor (7 years)

Joel Blauner

Morningside Homeowners Association—President

Mobile 999-999-9999

YiKES! ASSIGNMENT 9

Create Your Reference List

You must first contact any reference you use to get their permission. If they are willing to provide this service, explain how they can help you. You will want them to be able to reinforce some aspect of experience or competence critical to the role. Have them identified on your list by "type" with appropriate contact information.

YiKES! NUGGET

Connect All Parties on a Reference Request via Email

Another great idea is to confirm the reference request through email. Mark Morek suggests confirming the request by emailing back the recruiter, the company contact, and your reference(s). Include the references as a "carbon copy" (cc). This gets all parties synchronized and tips your reference(s) that they may be contacted. Better still, call your reference and confirm the message. The interview process can be hectic. This approach has proven helpful for organizations. It helps to leave a voicemail alerting and coaching your reference of a potential call if you cannot connect with them.

A Couple of Ideas and Good Habits to Start

YiKES! NUGGET

Organize Your Hard Drive

As you start to capture your career history and timeline, you will want to start a folder on your computer named "Resume." It will be used to store drafts, references lists, competencies tables, and other pertinent stuff. As you develop opportunities, you should capture them in subfolders organized by company name and subfolders by job title. Throughout your search, you will target different opportunities at the same company, so keep things organized. It will help keep you organized.

You should also consider capturing the results of your current position in a Word document kept in a file folder on your computer. Add wins and nuggets as they happen. Evaluate those successes every year. Capturing this data "real-time" is a great habit. And you are never too old to begin! Capturing wins as they are fresh will allow you to include enhanced details. These can give depth and color to a significant event or win by adding numbers, dollars, and percentages. They can also give you the confidence to create a "SOAR" story! They do not have to be formatted with any precision; just get them into the folder for future use.

YiKES! NUGGET

Update Your Resume Annually

It is a good practice to update your resume in conjunction with your annual performance review. Please set a private calendar reminder. Update your LinkedIn profile to keep it aligned with your resume.

Remember to accumulate the essence of your work, wins, and summaries in a folder on your laptop called "Resume." Do this as they occur throughout the year. You can refresh the resume annually, with every promotion or new assignment, or as suggested above at every annual performance review. Those are all perfect times. You can sanitize and package it at year-end.

Stay active on and maintain a current LinkedIn profile in alignment with your resume—they must match. Keeping your LinkedIn profile current allows you to be found in a search by a recruiter for a job that may be a good opportunity for

you. If you get the opportunity to apply for a job, take the time to optimize your resume with a keyword match analysis and then rewrite it for maximum effect.

The Resume—The Conclusion

So now, your resume has captured the essence of the *one-in-a-million you*! You have a Professional Summary that includes some type of compelling hook or catchphrase. You have listed your career in chronological order and have bullet points with numbers, dollars, and percentages to show the ***impact*** of your work. You have been sensitive to creating balance and have not blown the reader's mind with too many numbers. You use white space to make the document easy on the eyes and readable. Your education has been nicely summarized and is tidy.

You have contacted references, have created a list, and know how and when to work with them. You ordered good-looking, high-quality business cards and have created your vCard. You now have a greeting recorded on your cell phone voicemail. This is all great progress—take a moment to enjoy these advancements! You give yourself a competitive advantage when you incorporate the Yikes! Nuggets listed in this book.

A recent phenomenon impacting everyone is the growing awareness and use of artificial intelligence (AI) and ChatGPT (www.chatgpt.openai.com). Some of you may be using this site today. The problem with using AI to write a resume is if you don't feed it data that captures the size and scale of your work, you'll get another generic, bland resume. Worse, it will have an impersonal writing style – it won't be written in your voice. I don't recommend you become hooked on it. Developing your own resume will better reflect you. It is a process you can and will learn. With the entire 6-Step Process, you will get better over time and with practice.

Rest assured, you are working smartly, efficiently, and professionally! You are gaining a competitive advantage with the completion of every step. Next up is "Step 3: LinkedIn and Applying Online," where we will discuss how to optimize LinkedIn and provide more tips regarding applying online.

STEP 3

LINKEDIN AND APPLYING ONLINE

LinkedIn is the number-one database for hiring professionals and recruiters in search of talent.

Many online application processes enable you to post your resume or marketing brief via a hiring company's career opportunity portal or through a jobs aggregator such as CareerBuilder.com.

Both represent your career information 24/7/365 and must be current and accurate, but you also need to be careful not to get too caught up in applying online.

LinkedIn and Applying Online

These two topics are related as they are the digital representations of your career body of work.

When applying online, your salary history and requirements may be requested. In some instances, salary or compensation details are a requirement, and you must enter the complete details. However, you should never enter them into your LinkedIn profile. Never!

Your LinkedIn Profile

LinkedIn is the top website people use to search for talent. Therefore, you will want to make sure your profile is professional, complete, and current. Your resume and LinkedIn information must always be synchronized.

Many companies search LinkedIn profiles for specific criteria. This is often done with artificial intelligence (AI) software or by associates in HR. They seek specific attributes and career experiences such as:

- Job or assignment titles
- Company names
- Keywords
- Universities and degrees
- Military service
- Trade associations
- Certifications
- Volunteering associations
- Interests

Any aspect of your LinkedIn profile can become search criteria. These searches will employ filters to eliminate or rank LinkedIn profiles based on how complete they are. The more complete your profile, the better. Conversely, the less complete, the lower the rank. This means you will want to attain "All-Star" status, a LinkedIn classification, in time. Your LinkedIn status is derived by how many of these are (or aren't) in your profile:

- Photo
- Complete versus incomplete fields
- Typographical errors
- "Recommendations" you give and have received
- Low number of connections

Incomplete and sloppy profiles reflect on the person and are filtered out of searches. I have seen several specialists present guidelines on how to optimize your Linked In profile with the goal of attaining "All-Star" status. Here are some suggestions:

- Quality photo
  - Ask someone—preferably a professional—to take your phone; no selfies, no cutting off half an image from a prior photo, etc. Be sure your photo is recent.
  - If you ask a family member or friend to take it, make sure the photo appears well-lit and your face is in focus and is the featured item.
  - The picture should be a portrait for men in (at least) a sports coat and white-collared shirt, and, depending upon your title, wear a tie.
  - A suit and blouse are appropriate for women. Wear a moderate level of makeup in your photo.
  - Only you should be in the photo. No friends, family, or pets. I do not care how attractive your mate is, they shouldn't appear in your LinkedIn picture.
  - Note: Many (faith-based) job-seeker groups offer professionals who will take your photo for free.
- Have three to five competencies or skills listed.
- Have a way to be contacted both by email and cell number.
- If you have an appropriate personal business website, link to it.
- Include a brief summary of your career and interests with a novel, eye-catching headline such as "CRM Process Hawk," "Monster Data Analyst," or "Silo-Crushing Executive."
- Have a synopsis of your career and competencies and quickly tell your story.
- Have a secondary background photo of something related to your industry or the city skyline where you live.
- Make sure there are no spelling errors.
- Recommend at least three people and have at least three people recommend you.
- Connect with people regularly.

- Post something about your industry occasionally or on behalf of a past employer you left on good terms with.
- Follow companies you are interested in and would consider working at or investing in.
- Join industry or association groups you work in or are targeting.
- Follow companies or people you are interested in.
- Post or share a post occasionally of a positive human interest or industry article.
- Avoid any political statements or party affiliations.
- Avoid any comments—good or bad—about other people, and keep anything you post about a person or company positive.
- Use "Recommendations" to say something positive about an associate.

YiKES! ASSIGNMENT 10

Create or Update Your LinkedIn Profile

Let's quickly revisit some Yikes! nuggets: Make sure you have an appropriate email address, a killer resume, and your "Elevator Speech" down pat. You can post your resume when searching, but remove it once you've landed a job. Make sure you have a high-quality, professional photo, and try to adopt as many of the above-listed ideas as possible. You can have as much detail as you want in your LinkedIn profile as you want.

LinkedIn Recommendations

The Recommendations section is unique. It is a commentary from someone else about you. There is an "art" to how to request and obtain favorable recommendations.

YiKES! NUGGET

How to Request a Recommendations on LinkedIn

Please do not give someone an "assignment" when asking for a recommendation. We are all too busy. Rather, write a draft, send it to them, and ask them to consider submitting the recommendation on your behalf. It might seem awkward at first, but after you do a few and see the responses, you will get over any anxiety in asking.

The recommendation should reinforce a valuable experience or skill in which you are competent. Its content should not be left to chance. You are in control and will ultimately allow the recommendation to be posted (or not) to your profile.

Since getting recommended by others contributes to your overall LinkedIn rating, you should make it easy for someone to recommend you. Therefore, draft (i.e., ghostwrite) the recommendation statement for your associate to review and edit. Strategically write it to reinforce your story, then ask them if they would agree to post it. Of course, they can make any edits they want and then return it to you for review before adding it on LinkedIn. Do the heavy lifting for them and revise as needed while reinforcing what you want them to say. Make sure they have experience with you in this area. It must be genuine and real. Most folks will appreciate getting the request and appreciate that you did the bulk of the work. They may make a subtle edit before returning the recommendation, but keep in mind that you have the final say in posting in. It is your call.

There are countless books and YouTube videos and people out there who describe how to optimize LinkedIn. Many present online (i.e., Zoom, WebEx, etc.) or at job-seeker meetings and are free of charge. I'm not going to elaborate much more here as this is not my area of expertise; however, I know a complete profile is a critical aspect of job searching. You want a professional-looking profile.

Strive to attain an "All-Star" status. Your number of connections is important; fifty of them will trigger the "All-Star" achievement. This is a must for all, even college grads looking to enter the workforce. However, it must be professional. Therefore, no red Solo cups, friends, animals, or lingerie in the photos, people!

LinkedIn for Research

Before you get terribly excited about an opportunity, it is best to do some research on the company. Get some sense of the business's culture and the pros and cons of working there. Do your best to determine why the position is open. Was the employee promoted, transferred, or fired?

Patrick Fladung of the North Canton Executive Networking Group (NC ENG) believes ten hours of research per opportunity is the minimum requirement. This effort will give you a competitive advantage by preparing you better than all the other applicants. I know what you're thinking. Ten hours seems too long, right? However, considering you will need to research all the items below, such a time length is often appropriate. I held a mergers and acquisitions role at a large company for a year. During that assignment, we researched them to get a good sense of the company, its leadership, and business challenges, and issues. We looked for good and bad news and spent several full days on research. You will be surprised at what you will learn. Research will help you develop better questions to bring up at the interview (more on this later).

When researching a company it is helpful to make a list of information on topics such as:

- Financials:
  - Sales, expenses, operating income, and EBIT (earnings before interest and taxes) and its price to earnings (PE Ratio)—get a sense of the company's financial health.
- Governmental Issues:
  - What governmental phenomenon has recently or is impacting their business (i.e., the trend to renewable energy's impact on the oil and gas companies)?
- Environmental Impact:

- Is that company battling class-action lawsuits at present?
- Leadership:
  - Are the company's leaders stable or is there a revolving-door policy there? The latter indicates underlying business problem(s) the board of directors may be trying to address.
- Group or Division Trends:
  - In larger Fortune 500 companies, you will likely be joining a business unit. What is currently going on with them?
- The Hiring Team:
  - Research the people leading the business unit. Take notes on the ones you will likely meet. Use Google and LinkedIn during your research and speak with people about them to get a feel of who you will be interacting with.

I think it wise to speak with current and past employees—they are your best resources. Understand the culture and how they treat people. This is the best use of your time prior to a phone screen or interview. Make time in your job search daily to identify and attempt to speak with at least a few employees – this will be a challenge to gain access, but valuable. Most will not respond. It will take time to find those willing to discuss internal information about the company with you. Ask if there are challenging and/or bad managers in the area you are looking to join. Learning from an insider why the job is open is a good way to start a discussion. *You're evaluating the company and culture as much as they are interviewing you.*

A lack of understanding about the organizations I had joined proved to be a personal failing. Two bad experiences arose due to my incomplete research and I was let go after one year. At one business, I was part of a dysfunctional team with underperforming technology. The other was a political situation coupled with a peculiar team culture. Such short assignments spooked me. It made my work ethic and ability to hold a job look sketchy. In hindsight, there was, in fact, some positive that came from it. It gave me experiences I could draw upon when helping others. I take full responsibility for getting into these situations and strongly recommend you spend more time on researching prospective companies and cultures—a much better alternative than blindly applying to job opportunities online.

Reading articles online and reviews on job aggregator sites (i.e., Glassdoor.com, Indeed.com, theLadders.com, etc.) is helpful. However, nothing trumps speaking with people. You want to learn about "the admiral, the ship's captain, the first mate, and the rest of the crew" when considering your career journey. The goal is to get on the right boat, successfully contribute, and enjoy the voyage!

Glassdoor.com, Google and Yahoo! Financial News are good tools when researching as well. Any tidbit on the company, executives, key managers, and financial trends may prove valuable. The company's website will likely have a "Media and News Releases" section—another great resource. It is also a good place to find topics that will help you gain a better understanding of the company's strategy, plans for growth, and profitability. Why work to join a company invested in bad markets and that has a poor long-term financial outlook? Confirm they are making money and have a bright future. Scan their annual report too.

Many companies simply have insecure people. Some have dysfunctional and/or systemically bad cultures. They may have oppressive leaders, incompetent managers, or worse, toxic cultures not conducive to good morale and teamwork. Regardless of the compensation package, it is too much of a career risk to join a dysfunctional company. I learned that the hard way. I was well-compensated in those back-to-back, one-year assignments. So, keep in mind it is not all about the money!

Let's circle back to understanding why the position came open. Was the person fired or promoted? Why? Insights are gleaned when you engage in this topic. Find people who had the job! Get their perspective. Watch and listen for signals or "red flags," and do not drive through them! I did. Ugh!

I failed to research a company because I was desirous to stay in an industry I enjoyed. I jumped into a company that had two dysfunctional employees. I soon learned they had a corporate psychiatrist on staff, working with these individuals and their teams. It was so bad, the shrink suggested we read a book titled *101 Ways to Work with an A**hole and How to Succeed Anyway* by Lou Harry. We all struggled with these insecure and obnoxious people. Prospective customers did not want to work with them unless they had to. I had no idea what I had gotten myself into. I had failed to do adequate research. However, realize that no matter how in-depth your research, you might not be able to uncover all the potential pitfalls about an organization or its management. People, in general, do not give negative feedback, but you will be surprised what you can learn when you reach out. Research is key. Remember, more preparation time is required than actual interview time. Keep this in mind.

Research, network, and "ferret out" information regarding the opportunity you are considering! Take notes. Use the information as the basis for questions to ask on the phone screen or during an interview. We dive deeper in "Step 4: Phone Screens and Interviews."

YiKES! ASSIGNMENT 11

Research a Company Where You Will Be Interviewed

So, you're now at the point where you're ready to research target companies or any company that may contact you for a phone screen or interview. First, get a keyword match analysis of your resume compared to the job description from www.jobscan.com. Confirm how you would be a good fit. Then research the company and culture while learning about the needs of the company. This will help you prepare your questions for them. Get a sense of how the position impacts the company's goals or mission. No matter the level, every job should have some connection to the overall strategic goals of that business. Make the connection. Bringing up and inquiring as to these ideas will separate you from the pack and raise your perceived value. Be a problem-solver!

Don't forget to contact personnel as described above and compile notes while doing so as these will help you prepare for the phone screen or interview.

Once you are satisfied this is a company you wish to consider working at, only then should you pursue the opportunity. Your research should include:

- Company profile and mission statement
- Publicly traded information—ticker symbol, revenue, profitability trends,

price/earnings ratio, dividends paid (percent, history), cash flow, recent divestitures, or acquisitions

- Industry sector information—trends and health/governmental impact
- Financial health information—relative to the company's sector. Are they a leader, challenger, or laggard?
- Environmental (and legal) issues
- Leadership team breakdown: president, chief technology officer, chief financial officer, VP of Sales, VP of Manufacturing, etc. How long have they all worked there? Are they committed or carpetbaggers?
- Hiring manager information—What's their educational background? How many years have they served in the company under this title, etc.?
- Past employees—How would they rate the company?
- Present employees—gain their input as well
- People who worked in the job you are considering—such insights will help you gain an edge regarding that company's expectations
- Other pertinent issues—you will surely uncover more details as you research the above categories

This type of research will better prepare you for a phone screen and an interview. You will clearly stand out from the crowd and be seen in a positive light if you come armed with these nuggets of information and questions. Further, you will have vetted the company, confirming it is financially healthy. Get the flow here? You are being more selective in your approach and remaining critically honest with yourself throughout the process. If it is a bad culture or a poorly performing business, or you are not a good fit, fuhgeddaboudit!

Applying Online

Applying online is a necessary evil. It is one of the single biggest things you will learn to understand and optimize. Huge warning here: It is very dangerous. Yes, dangerous. In a job search, it can devolve into a lonely time where folks get inwardly focused and start breathing in too much of their own exhaust. This can trigger a spiral downward due to a lack of perceived progress and lead to depression. The process can seem hopeless at times. However, don't forget that old cliché I mentioned back at the beginning, "It's a marathon not a sprint" rings as true as ever! This is a major reason why I suggest you set a goal to contact two to three industry associates per day and have a *conversation* with them! You need person-to-person connectivity during your job search.

Applying online can also be a severe waste of time. You can spend a few—or several—hours creating an online profile and answering a myriad of questions. You think you are making progress. However, this can be a false sense of achievement. Especially after completing several of these and not getting any feedback. Plus, your efforts may actually never even get read by a human! If you're reaching for a position that you're not qualified for (experience, education, etc.) it's true – no one may read your application. The ATS software will filter you out.

Applying online can be a necessity, however. Perhaps you were referred into the organization, had a discussion with HR, and they required you to "apply online." This may necessitate creating an online profile in a clunky software system. This can take an hour or more, based on your work history and the website. Yes, you must recreate your career, chronologically, in their database—effectively rewriting your resume. Yuck! There is no quick way to do it. Some of the more advanced systems will parse your resume (as a Word document) and auto-populate the info. Then all you will need to do is edit the info. Hooray!

However, more often than not, the process will be very time-consuming. You will want to be critical when beginning the effort. So, be sure to ask yourself: Are you truly qualified for the job?

Another consideration is the company. If you really want to work at a specific company but the fit is not strong, you can take a gamble and get into their database by applying. This will get you on their radar for other positions if your education and experiences meet their minimum requirements. I know companies that hire engineers for everything. Ugh!

YiKES! NUGGET

Avoid the "Time-Trap" of Blindly Applying Online

Simply applying online with one generic resume is a dangerous "time trap." You think you are increasing your chances of a connection; however, you are lulling yourself into a false sense of achievement. The chances of getting contacted by using a resume not customized to the position are low. There are too many other people doing the same thing. This is why companies use software to screen out low-probability candidates.

Due to the sheer volume of applicants a company can receive, they will typically set filters using software that reduces or eliminates the chance of a human being actually viewing the application. The applicant thus has wasted valuable job-search time.

- Be selective and carefully consider jobs to apply for as the application process can take hours.
- Be prepared as most organizations—whether you've been referred or not—require you to apply online.
- If the fit is not optimal, do not bother—you will never get a call. Do not waste your time unless the company is a target and this is an attempt to get on their radar.
- Keep in mind that this time would be better spent networking and speaking to people who know you and what you can do.

YiKES! NUGGET

How to List Salary Requirements
When Requested While Applying Online

Another challenge when applying online is questions on past wages or salary and/or your expected salary. These are filters used to rule out people expecting a salary above what is budgeted. This supports the long-standing negotiation rule "He who names a number first loses." Unfortunately, by setting a salary expectation, you risk pricing yourself out of the job *or* leaving money on the table—going under value. Therefore, try entering a text (alpha), not a number, in the salary requirement field. You can use phrases such as:

- Negotiable

- Competitive

- Market

- In-line with industry

Be honest if a numeric response is mandatory. Base it on your budgetary requirements. Hey, if they cannot pay what you need, it's not a good opportunity for you. There is a greater risk of pricing yourself out of consideration as most "shoot big."

I've also entered "$0" to get through the application process when a number is required. Sometimes this is accepted. Sometimes, a number greater than $0 is required. Either way, if you can get through this question without defining a salary, great. This opens the door for a dialogue. I've had HR reps call and ask about my compensation requirements. This opens the door to make remarks such as "I know 'ABC Global' is a high-quality company and will offer a market competitive-level salary and compensation plan." You can also try this approach:

"If you are interested in making me an offer, please do. I'll advise if the salary and benefits package will work for my family and me." Try these approaches. Do not give out a number unless it is absolutely required. When you do, make it real.

You should know your salary minimum requirement. This is critical and should be a function of your budget. Determine what you will require for living expenses after all taxes, healthcare contributions, and the 401K minimum contribution percentage to determine your salary requirement. Depending upon the position level, there may also be non-salary compensation elements to define: a sign-on bonus, sales/quota bonus, 401K match, commission, stock grants, etc. You need to understand the total compensation package. Understand your budget. Define what your "walk away" salary requirement will be. As painful as it might be, it may be best to pass on the opportunity. Yikes!

If you are asked to sign an "employment contract," I suggest you seek professional advice from someone who specializes in such contracts.

Applying online is necessary with many companies. In most instances, these organizations will ask you to upload your resume. You now know, it is imperative to take the time to do a keyword match and write a compelling, unique Professional Summary for a given opportunity. These minor "tweaks" will help. If writing is not your strong suit, have someone write it with you. Or hire a service. Collaboration is key as none of us individually are smarter than all of us combined! A compelling Professional Summary may be the single most important element on your resume. It can motivate the reader to read more. Your career summary and, of course, your body of work must be appropriate to the job description. Fishing trips, taking long shots, and applying way above your experience level—or applying to opportunities in which you do not meet the requirements—are a waste of time.

As previously mentioned, the importance of a high correlation of keywords in the job description to those in your resume (and when applying online) cannot be overstated. Keywords must be in your resume and translate into the online application. Remember to use www.jobscan.com to get a keyword match percentage and list of the keywords that must be used to optimally match to the job. To use jobscan.com, simply paste a copy of the job description and a copy of your resume into the site. Within a few seconds, you will get the results.

One of the NC ENG volunteers I've worked with has a novel approach to determining keywords. Patrick Fladung recommends you review five different job descriptions for similar positions (i.e., senior auditor, sales manager, tax accountant, etc.) from five different companies. Review them and determine the keywords in each description and then use those in your resume—when applying for such jobs.

LinkedIn and Applying Online—in summary:

LinkedIn

LinkedIn is the number-one database employers use when searching for talent. You should maintain a professional appearance on your profile and take steps to achieve "All-Star" status. It is critical you have a professional photo as this reinforces your professional persona. There are plenty of experts and "how-to" videos available on how best to optimize LinkedIn. I recommend you view some or seek out these experts who often present to job-seeker groups for free. You can attend a presentation in-person or via Zoom online events. I recommend you maintain your profile at least annually or as career changes occur. Awards, certifications, a new hairstyle, or a change of job should trigger an update too.

LinkedIn is a great tool to use for researching potential companies and associates and to learn about potential managers. Ask about the culture. How do they treat employees? This is a key aspect of working at a company versus finding a great company. Yahoo! Finance, Glassdoor.com, and the ubiquitous Google are good research tools.

Applying Online

Be very judicious regarding how much time you spend applying online. There is a risk you will waste time that could be better spent speaking with people who know you and what you can do. Let them know you are a "free agent" looking for opportunities.

Avoid entering a salary requirement when applying online unless it is absolutely mandatory. There is a risk of pricing yourself out of consideration *or* leaving money on the table.

You want your application to tell a compelling story that connects your skills and experience to the needs expressed in the job description. It is not about your goals but rather about how you address their needs.

You now understand the challenges of applying online. It is much more time-consuming than simply "clicking on" a job opportunity on LinkedIn or elsewhere. Be wary of avoiding "blind" attempts to apply for jobs, and know you are far better off connecting with people on the phone or otherwise speaking to people to get the ball rolling and make things happen.

Whew, there is a lot to be aware of regarding LinkedIn and applying online. Now you know a lot of the insider secrets that separate a successful job-seeker from one who's just spinning their wheels! Take a moment to savor how enlightened you now are!

STEP 4

PHONE SCREENS AND INTERVIEWS

Phone screens are discussions used to determine whether you qualify enough to advance to an in-person or online interview. The interview is your chance to convince the organization you're the best candidate for the position.

Research, preparation, and practice are "mission critical" to success at this point in the job-seeking process.

Phone Screens and Interviews

You have now researched the industry and the target company that has presented an opportunity. You have spoken with some folks who currently work or have worked there. You confirmed your background is genuinely a good fit, given their needs listed in the job description. You are convinced they have a healthy culture. You painstakingly wrote a compelling Professional Summary tailored to the job description. You confirmed you have a high keyword match.

You networked and learned a little bit about the hiring manager and got positive feedback. Your research exposed some headwinds the company is facing, and you are prepared to discuss them. You worked a connection to get your resume in front of the HR screener, and because your background is such a good fit, they want to speak with you! Good—you're successfully advancing through the **6-Step Process**!

Now it is either time for a scheduled phone screen or an in-person interview. Congratulations! Nervous? I hope so. If you are not, something ain't right!

No, most folks do not research enough or even prepare for a phone screen or an interview. Let us address why adequate preparation is critical and greatly increases the chances for a positive outcome—an offer for employment!

Macro-Phenomenon Regarding Phone Screens and Interviews

A good phone screen—or interview—goes both ways. There are two sides to every coin. The company will interview you as a candidate, but you should likewise interview the company to determine if you want to work there. Job one is to demonstrate you can address their needs, but job two is to determine if the company is a long-term fit for your career goals. Think of such a discussion as a dialogue versus a "grilling."

Like a sales call, more time should be spent preparing for a phone screen or an interview than executing it! Digest that. Proper preparation will give you confidence and the ability to express yourself in the best possible manner. You owe it to yourself and your family to adequately prepare.

Always choose quality over the quantity. As expressed in "Step 3: LinkedIn and Applying Online," when preparing for a phone screen or interview, you will want to research the company. Speak with associates current and past, and even ask their customers what they think of the company. Find out if they know the hiring manager and/or your potential manager.

Research the associates related to that company whom you will speak with on LinkedIn. Note their career progression and some of their job titles. Note where they went to college. These topics can be good "icebreakers." You want them to lead the discussion, but you can always restart a stalled conversation by drawing on the research. "When I researched your background, I found you attended LSU. Why did you choose LSU?" This will also send a positive signal that you took some time to *do* research, which will reflect well on your level of profession-alism. Just do not ask about why Nick Saban left LSU and his subsequent success at Alabama!

YIKES! NUGGET

Plan to Interview the Company

You will gain a lot of critical information about the company, how they treat people, and the culture (nurturing or otherwise) by asking questions during the interview. This is not a one-way discussion. Not many people understand this. Therefore, you will separate yourself from the other candidates in a positive way by asking well-conceived questions.

YIKES! ASSIGNMENT 12

Create Your Interview Questions

Develop a list of questions to address industry, company, and position issues based on your research. Plan to weave them into the discussion. Have them typed and double spaced with plenty of room to take notes. You should under-stand the industry and health of the company. You want to learn how they treat people. You want to understand if they view the culture as nurturing of associates.

During the interview, take calculated notes – but don't transcribe the conversation. Write down the big points and any "Ah-ha" insights that arrive along the way. You might pick up some info to review with the recruiter afterward, along with issues to further research. I suggest six to eight very focused questions for a scheduled sixty-minute interview. More questions are appropriate for longer interviews. If you are invited for half of or a full day of interviews, have the question sheet ready for all the potential people you will meet with. Keep several copies handy as you should ask these questions to each person or panel group you interview with.

YiKES! NUGGET

Answer the Question Asked and Address the Needs Listed in the Job Description

My best advice is to answer the question asked—do not volunteer more information than what is necessary to supply the information requested. Give the interviewer(s) time to process your answers. Stay quiet and let them take notes. This is very important. Be comfortable with some silence during an interview.

Treat the discussion like a "first date." The phone screen, or interview, is the only chance to make a first impression. The in-person interview is an indication that they are closer to considering you by investing in the face-to-face time (either in person or via a virtual interview). In either case, they are making a time investment on your behalf. Do not let them regret it!

These discussions are an opportunity to convey to them that you are *the* answer to their problems! Remember, it is *always* about how you address their needs as expressed in the job description! Continuously circle back to address their needs, even when they are asking about your experiences. They should be relevant to their needs. This is an excellent time to validate whether the job description is current or if new issues have arisen that they need to address—needs that were not in the description. Do not be obnoxious (that goes without saying) if new things (needs) are thrown at you. Simply keep their needs at the forefront of your mind. Do not let your pride lead you to crow about your successes unless they are germane to the need. Convey you have the experience and skills they are after.

I'll refer to the phone screen and the interview as the "interview" going forward. The main points are similar in either case, with some unique aspects relating to the in-person interview that will be addressed toward the end of the section.

When preparing for the interview, you must:

- Research the company website "media and news" areas, annual report, the local newspaper where they are headquartered for articles, etc.
- Research potential managers you will meet—one or more of them may become your new manager(s)!
- Practice asking and answering questions with a friend and ask them to critique you.
- Ask why the position came open. Was it due to a promotion or something else?
- Answer only the question asked and then enjoy the silence as interviewers process answers and take notes.
- Keep answers to ninety seconds or less – and feel free to ask the interviewer if they'd like to expand an answer in greater detail – that could require more time.
- Confirm you have answered their question completely – to their satisfaction.
- Weave in a "SOAR" story wherever applicable.
- Dress well and appropriately for the position and culture—even for a Skype interview.

Dressing appropriately for a Skype interview will make a good impression. It will also serve to keep you well-aware of the importance of the situation, or "Up, on top of the wheel," to use a stock car racing analogy. Not interviewing in person is no excuse to be casual in appearance, or worse, too casual in your approach. You'll carry yourself better dressed up.

Practice, Practice, Practice...

Practice is very important. Talking about oneself can feel foreign to some people. You will be discussing your skills, successes, and how they apply to the prospective employer. Plan to weave in what you want to learn or skill(s) you want to develop while in the role. This shows maturity and self-confidence and that you are forward-thinking. However, be sensitive to not expose an area in which you know you are not as strong as they may require. An example would be if the job listing states that seven years of experience are required, but you have five.

My wife says the person who does the most talking while on a date has the better time. He/she then perceives whether the date was a success. There is a parallel between a date and an interview. The people interviewing you (or the one asking the majority of the questions while on a date) will likely be the one determining whether they will "take a next step". You need to be prepared to let them speak, ask questions, answer your questions, and, most importantly, let them maintain control. Seek quiet passages during the discussion—enjoy the silence.

Employ active listening techniques. Be prepared to fully concentrate on what is being communicated to you. Clarify ideas or questions if required. Do not quickly respond. Rather, process the information before you answer. Be thoughtful. You should want to ask questions about their industry, the company, and the position.

Your questions for the interviewer(s) should require more than a yes or no answer. Questions should begin with "Who," "What," "Where," "When," and "How." Examples include: "What are the top competitive issues the company is facing?" "Which technologies are the company investing in and why?" "Where do you see the company in three years?" Open-ended questions allow interviewers to share their knowledge and give you insights. You should take notes as well.

Practicing beforehand is not just important but also a necessity for a successful interview. I recommend you practice the interview at least twice with someone: a friend, spouse, someone else you respect, another job-seeker, and/or a volunteer who assists job-seekers. You must ask for, and trust, that you will receive candid, constructive criticism and feedback.

You need honest criticism about your performance. How is your answer content, answer length, body language, posture, eye contact, dress, and overall countenance? Are you appropriately confident, for example? This question and others need to be critically addressed. No time for Mr. Nice Guy. One of the most experienced interviewing coaches of the North Canton Executive Networking Group (NC ENG), Patrick Fladung. He is known to dole out "tough love." He is extremely thoughtful yet critical regarding what is said, how it is said, and often, what is not said. An interesting warning, he preaches, is to avoid exposing an experience gap or an area of potential concern (i.e., age). You will want to be yourself. But be the best, prepared version of yourself. Some "Behavioral and Situational Questions" are listed later in the book.

YiKES! ASSIGNMENT 13

Practice an Interview

I'll assume that at this point, you have done your homework, and you have a phone screen or interview lined up on a real opportunity. Get with a trusted friend, utilize the numbered list below, and practice.

1. Create a list of questions for your interview partner to ask (see the list in the section below).
2. Create a list of questions you would like to ask the interviewer(s)—for practice, write down possible answers ahead of time to these questions and refer to them.
   a. Base some of those questions on your research of the company and industry. For example:
      i. What's the number-one challenge for the company?

    ii. What are some industry challenges?

    iii.How does this position address these phenomena?

  b. Base some of those questions on the job being offered. For example:

    i. Why is the job open—promotion or other?

    ii. What are the top three skills or attributes you value most for the role?

    iii.What would success look like in this job after six months? A year?

  c. Do not ask one of your prepared questions if it has already organically come up in the interview!

3. Practice answering the questions with someone as you must articulate aloud your responses to get the most benefit from the mock interview. I recommend:

  a. Going through the entire question set while taking notes the first time around.

  b. Review and critique as soon as the first mock interview ends.

  c. Make sure your practice partner provides fair criticism. Put on your "thick skin." Remember: This is designed to make you better! Make sure they understand.

  d. Answer each question and then enjoy the silence. Your interviewing partner can help you focus here by taking some time to jot down notes, emulating the experience.

4. Practice the interview a second time. I recommend:

  a. Using the same questions.

  b. Incorporating the fine-tuned answers you have developed.

  c. Keeping your answers shorter, crisp, and to the point. This establishes better pacing with more quiet time between each answer.

5. Practice a third time if you can. Once on a roll, you will undoubtedly want to further refine your answers. This is a confidence-building process. I recommend:

  a. Going through the complete list of prepared questions.

  b. Addressing only the big issues—and, hopefully, there are few of those.

  c. Completing at least one full mock interview, including ending statements and a handshake (or a fist bump or other pandemic-appropriate gesture).

Unique Aspects of an In-Person Interview

In an in-person interview, you'll find the rules slightly different. First off, remember to be yourself. Be the true you. However, be prepared through research and practice to be your *best self* during an in-person interview.

You want to be dressed appropriately. Fit the culture; however, I recommend a suit and tie if you are not sure – especially for an office-based position. Most interview coaches suggest dressing quite well, meaning a business (formal) suit and tie for men with a suit and a blouse for women. You have only one opportunity to make a first impression. If working with a recruiter, follow their recommendation. They may know the culture. If not, do some research. Wear a suit and tie if appropriate or a sports coat and open-collar shirt—or jeans and a polo shirt—if that is the company norm. Strive to be the best-dressed person they will see the day of your visit, but appropriately so. If this requires investing in a new suit, do it! Conventional wisdom suggests a navy-blue or light gray suit makes the best impression. It is also recommended to minimize contrasts and clashing colors. To play it safe, wear a white shirt or blouse. This makes coordinating a tie or an accessory piece (i.e., a scarf or brooch) easier. For men, matching your tie to the suit works best with a bright white shirt, though I often see light tan or light blue shirts for technical folks (i.e., engineers). A silk tie with a woven pattern is preferred, and a coordinated color scheme is always best. You cannot go wrong with a bright white shirt or blouse.

Some resources that offer more information on this topic are included in the Reference Section.

YiKES! NUGGET

First Impressions Matter and Interview Execution Tips

Whether online or in-person, dress appropriately. You have only one chance to make a first impression. If unsure of the culture, men should wear a tie. For women, a nice white blouse and suit is recommended if you have to err on the side of dressing to the max.

Have a firm but not crushing handshake. Engage high on the vertex between the thumb and forefinger. No clammy, dead-fish hand-shakes permitted!

- A fist or elbow bump may be appropriate in the pandemic age, but if the associate extends their hand, shake it!

- Carry some hand sanitizer with you if you have concerns about the spread of germs.

Look them in the eye and say, "Pleased to meet you, [their name]. My name is..."

Let the interviewer or panel of interviewers set the tone. Allow them to break the ice because:

- This reinforces they are in control of the discussion, not you.

- It is about their needs and not your career goals (beyond your excellent fit).

- If they are awkwardly quiet, do not fret. It is early in the "date." Just enjoy the silence.

- You are subordinate to everything in the process.

The company has pain points as outlined in the job description. You are going to be asked how your skills address them, so:

- Discuss them as naturally as you can, but make sure every answer is short and sweet!

- Answer the specific question asked and do not volunteer additional info until asked. When asked use an applicable SOAR story.

- Manage the information flow. If you have ever listened to air traffic control (sometimes an in-flight audio option) they are highly efficient and on-point, with little or no extra information offered. They do this to not confuse the pilots and "crowd" the frequency. Think efficient communication.

- Do not confuse the interviewer(s) with too much information or noise. Just answer the question asked.

As discussed in "Step 2: The Resume," have a "SOAR" story (**S**ituation, **O**bservations made, **A**ctions taken, and the **R**esults achieved quantified in dollars and percentages) ready to go. To best ensure success, follow the steps outlined below:

- Have one or two well-rehearsed SOAR stories developed and be ready for them to ask, "Is there anything else you would like to tell us about yourself?" When they do, share the most appropriate SOAR story if you have not already. Incorporate a response based on what you have learned during the interview as they will appreciate being "listened to."

- If neither of your two SOAR stories is appropriate, you can pass. It is a situational thing, but I'd err on the side of trying to get at least one of your successes into the conversation. Explain the IMPACT you made.

- However, do not push a SOAR story as sometimes they simply do not fit. Forcing them to listen to something not on-point will likely become awkward.

You should bring questions to the interview.

Have questions prepared in advance based on your research. Inquire about the industry (trends), the company (challenges), and the position (impact to the company).

Some good questions are:

- What's the near-term most significant challenge for the company?
- How does it impact the job for which I'm applying?
- Why do people want to join the company?
- What's the company's single greatest challenge?
- How does this position address this?
- Why is this position open?
- If it is an existing opening, what happened to the person in the role?

- What industry, economic, and/or social trends are impacting the company?
- What is the environment or culture like?
- Are there concerns about the direction of the company?
- How are the managers treated by leadership?
- How do managers treat the employees?
- What else do you think is important for me to know about the company?
- Would you encourage a family member to work here?

Always conclude an interview with these thoughts and *ask for the job* **following these guidelines:**

- Ask if there was anything not answered to their satisfaction. Example: "Is there a barrier to hiring me?"
- Open the floor to any issues they haven't addressed by saying something to the effect of: "I'd like to make sure there are no outstanding issues or information gaps before I leave today."
- Reinforce your qualifications. You can say, "I sense I'm a good fit," then thank them for their time and advise them that "I would like to join your team" and/or, *"I appreciate your consideration and want the job!"*

It is amazing how so many people do not ask for the job or express openly to join the team. Confirm **"I would like to join the team and want the job!"**

I must reinforce this most critical aspect of concluding a positive interview. You want to reinforce how you are equipped to meet their needs, but do not overdo it. *Ask for the job!* Say you want to join the team. Be sure to also mention that you look forward to the challenges involved in the offered job! Recruiters, volunteers, and interview coaches all reinforce this critical advice. You owe it to yourself and your family to *please ask for the job!*

My Worst Interview

I bombed a panel interview at a large, on-highway truck parts manufacturer. It went so badly. I can only laugh at myself upon reflection. I had a false sense of confidence because I had met their president at a trade show. I felt we were "simpatico," had become "fast friends," and had developed a good comfort level with each other. I read too much into my time with him. I had learned that they had a position in their aftermarket parts group for a sales manager.

I networked into the company and organized an interview. The sales manager position required my skill set and background. I was a solid fit. but was overconfident. I failed to research them adequately. I never asked the sales director (who arranged the interview) for insights into their "tribal behaviors" and/or culture. I did not ask anything about the president such as "Is he chatty and laid back or black and white? A by-the-numbers, no small-talk guy?" Nothing.

I did not think to ask where the president ranked on the DiSC continuum either. If you are unaware of this, please see the DiSC Personality Traits Test in the Reference. It is a way to learn about someone's personality traits so you can relate to them in a style in which *they* are comfortable. In principle, people tend to interact with others based on one or possibly two of these four behavioral constructs:

- **Dominance:** direct, strong-willed, and forceful
- **Influence:** sociable, talkative, and lively
- **Steadiness:** gentle, accommodating, and soft-hearted
- **Conscientiousness:** private, analytical, and logical

Understanding these personalities and how to relate to them is very helpful in a job search. It is a great tool we use in consultative technical selling—to approach people the way *they* want to be treated, in a manner comfortable for *them*. This is in stark contrast to the saying, "Treat people the way *you* want to be treated." That is an outdated approach.

Back to my bad interview. I walked into the interview blind. I was too chatty and offered too much additional information relative to the questions asked. I was long-winded in my answers. I literally said during the interview "I think I'm talking too much" and then did the Doctor Evil (of the *Austin Powers* movies) gesture of biting a knuckle. Yes, I actually did this during the interview! After the interview, I learned from the HR person that the president did not like "chatty" salespeople. What a schmuck I was!

I rated my performance an "F." I asked the HR contact whether I should circle back in six months for further consideration and was told no. No future consideration for employment at this leading enterprise—a result I had clearly earned and deserved. Did I mention that I was a schmuck?

In contrast to my bad interview, Charles Henle, a recent graduate of the Rochester Institute of Technology (RIT), aced a series of very challenging interviews. He had applied for a sales role in an IT systems security and software company. Charles is quite a unique person. In addition to earning a mechanical engineering degree from prestigious RIT, he co-founded a 501c3 charitable organization while in school called The Shore Foundation, which repurposes computers to donate to the city of Rochester and other organizations in need. When I think back to what I was doing in college... Well, let us move on!

He made it through three successful interviews. Charles reinforced how his ability to think had been honed at RIT and how his interests and skills were a good fit for the challenges of the job. Finally, he got to a one-on-one interview with the VP of Sales. The VP asked a classic question encountered by many prospective sellers out there: "Sell me something."

Charles was initially stunned. But he thought "on his feet." His mind immediately went to something he knew: The Shore Foundation. He proceeded to review the mission statement, explained the organization's objectives, and then *asked* the VP of Sales for support—the proverbial "asking for the order" during the interview. He got a commitment from the VP to donate to the organization. More importantly, he got the job! Charles had risen to the challenge when the VP had invited him to "Sell me something." In doing so, he had demonstrated a command of a topic and had been natural and confident. He got two commitments—a "two-fer"—on an interview! Brilliant!

This story reinforces the need to be yourself. I define selling as "Motivating someone to do something they otherwise would not do." Charles was able to motivate the VP to donate computers—an action he would not have otherwise taken. The discussion convinced the VP to hire Charles for a consultative selling and new business development role based in New York City! This also reinforces proper preparation and research. We had discussed questions to be ready for and to ask in advance. Charles was prepared and confident and was able to be himself during the interview.

I have shared this example of an interviewer challenging a job-seeker to "Sell me something" to reinforce a key point for interviews: always be yourself! *No one knows you better than you! No one knows your SOAR stories.*

Be ready to answer this classic interview question as well: "Why do you consider yourself a good candidate for the position?" This is common and applies to any role. You should answer by linking three requirements of the job to your experience and skill set. Connect your qualifications to the key requirements—make one or two clear connections to the needs of the position. Since you have practiced the interview a few times, you should by now be comfortable doing so quickly. Then, quietly let the interviewer digest and jot down notes.

Background Checks

Depending upon the industry, a formal background check may be a condition of employment. These are sourced from service providers who do this work very thoroughly. Some jobs, for example in the security industry, may require a drug screen and a polygraph ("lie detector") test. Most companies will have you perform a drug screen that includes a urine and/or hair sample screen. Tests can search for marijuana, opioids, and/or heroine. There is a plenty of information available online regarding drug screens and what is tested. I refer you to the National Institute on Drug Abuse in the Reference section under "Drug Screens References."

For those of you who have been employed for an extended period at one employer that does not use a random drug screen, you will need to consider the consequences of a drug screen with your new potential employer. Because if you use "pot" or other recreational drugs, be aware. Candidates that fail a drug screen will almost assuredly not be offered employment.

Drug use is disappointing for a variety of reasons. If you are serious about getting a job, and drug use is presently an addiction or recreation of yours, please seek help. Drug screens are becoming more popular as they mitigate risk for employers. Depending upon your situation, you may have to detox, clean up, and consider getting tested—all before you apply for a job. Only when clean should you start the process. You do not want a failed drug screen on record at a company you could work at. Do not get into a situation where you could blow a chance to join a great organization.

A Real Situation

I counseled Maxwell, a seasoned capital equipment seller in California. At his organization, he is also an expert in the machine tool industry where, through "subtractive manufacturing," a cutting tool removes material from a chunk of aluminum, titanium, or some other exotic alloy. This process is used to make components for aircraft frames, actuation systems, landing gear, or parts for gas turbine ("jet") engines. He sells these machines, which are known as "capital equipment"—a niche area of expertise. I got to know Max when he expressed interest in working with my employer. I learned some interesting things about his background. First, he was not a degreed engineer, which meant we would not hire him. Second, he had an issue that made coaching him more challenging.

Max had not one but two misdemeanor DUIs for driving under the influence (of alcohol), a real showstopper for companies that put sellers in company cars or who were expected to travel on business in their own vehicle. This was a liability risk best mitigated by not hiring the individual. Thankfully, when we connected (he reached out via LinkedIn), the DUIs were over seven years old. He was taking legal action to have them expunged from the public records. I learned that there are felony or misdemeanor DUI violations. Some of which can be removed from your public record. However, there are (evil) companies that exist with the express purpose of keeping this information alive. They extort money from you in exchange for removing your mug shot and associated records removed from their database. "Digital does not die" as they say. There are services, such as www.reputationdefender.com, that can help with social media issues. They sanitize your online digital records. If you are in such a situation, you will need to pursue corrective action. Do so before you start your search. Removal can take months.

For the record, it is best not to get behind the wheel when you are at risk for a DUI. Just call Uber, Lyft, or a cab. Better yet, just avoid alcohol when responsible for driving.

Let's get back to Maxwell, who had to decide whether to disclose the DUI during interviews. I've researched this enough to say, should you have a similar item in your background, you must seek legal counsel to address it. The resolution can be different based on the infraction, city, and state in which you live.

In some states, the counties will provide background information dating "back" to seven years. Others divulge information regardless of how old it is. Still others release info based on the compensation level of the position. In some instances, a $75,000-per-year salary can trigger a release. Disclosure can be managed very differently. Therefore, you should review the circumstances with legal counsel before your background check blows up a deal. Find an expert. I strongly advise you hire a lawyer. You may need to both remove the history from your record and determine how to appropriately address it in an interview. Seek out the best, most informed advice!

Basically, plan for a citation to show up on a background check employment verification. If it is not serious, you should own and disclose it. A felony will be found and brought to your attention anyway. If only a misdemeanor infraction, depending upon when and where it happened and the nature of the infraction, it may not need to be disclosed. If you have not looked for employment for an extended period of time because you have been employed throughout that period, you must invest in a discussion with legal counsel. There is too much at stake.

You may be asked, "Is there anything else in your background you want us to know about prior to us requesting a background check?" In the digital age, with so many ways to keep public information alive, it may be best to acknowledge an indiscretion. Address and own it. Explain the situation and charge, along with the corrective action(s) taken to date. You want to get it on and off the table quickly. Then get back to reinforcing how your experience, skills, and competencies address their needs.

Sexual Harassment

In my industrial technical sales career, we would sell "value-added services" that help improve process equipment reliability. We redesigned and upgraded equipment to extend the "mean time between repair" (MTBR). In this environment, most of the contact was with "grizzled" men, many of whom came up from the "school of hard knocks" (i.e., progressed up from a general labor role) to become managers of maintenance departments with multimillion-dollar budgets. Foul language, off-color jokes, and calendars of bikini-clad (or less) women were commonplace.

The industry is changing from a "good ole' boys" network dominated by men. Women are now commonly found in maintenance tech, management, and sales roles calling on manufacturing customers.

Fred, an experienced and highly respected technical seller, worked in Ohio. He tended to let old-school moirés get the best of him and was often insensitive around women co-workers. There was always an undercurrent of frustration or flat-out "I can't stand that guy," combined with an eye roll, expressed by his female associates. His customers appreciated Fred, however, and would look the other way regarding his insensitive behavior because he was so helpful, extremely knowable, and hard-working. They called Fred around the clock, on weekends and holidays, and he would always respond. He was very valuable to their operations.

Fred asked Ann Marie, a new addition to the company and a relatively young and attractive female seller, to join him on a sales call. He asked her to demonstrate a time-saving tool. After Ann Marie showed him how to use the device, Fred said, "See? It is so easy to use, even the pretty lady could use it!" She perceived this as a form of sexual harassment, though Fred said it had been a compliment. She filed a sexual harassment complaint against him. That became "strike one" in his personnel file.

Then came a second incident involving Fred and Ann Marie. They were discussing the best way to get a better discount from a supplier. In the industrial space, as in many industries, distributors often coax discounts out of their partners by sharing competitive information (about one against another). This is due to the ability to "switch" or substitute between suppliers the distributors represent. These products can have essentially the same "form, fit, and function". Think flat washers, nuts, and bolts. On the surface, they seem totally switchable; however, metallurgy and production standards suggest that this is not always the case.

When manufacturers sell through distributors, they often rely on such channels for information regarding an opportunity. Market price, which brands are acceptable, and other information is shared confidentially. Distributors choose to share competitive information when they have competing lines to get a lower price. Vendors are allowed, by law, to meet the competitive price if they want to. Friendships are made as this dialogue allows the distributor to either lower the resale price (to secure an order) or to increase their profit margin. Sometimes both.

In the second situation, Ann Marie was very happy to report that she had negotiated a better deal from a vendor. To which Fred said, "Way to go!" She then said, "He is traveling with me today and will be coming into the office in a minute, should you want to thank him." Fred said, regarding another potential opportunity, "Then why not take him in the back and 'beat him down' for another deal?" Ann Marie thought it was a veiled sexual reference. Thus, strike two went into his file, and Fred was terminated for sexual harassment!

Fred was a top seller with over twenty-five years of exemplary performance. He was fired for sexual harassment...for a comment taken out of context. Fred was devastated, ashamed, and humbled. He was now out of work in his fifties with an unseemly event on his file. Through a referral, I spoke with Fred and did some research on his behalf. A North Canton Executive Networking Group volunteer, Mike Ziarko, said it best: "He has to own it and take a corrective action to address it. Take a course to understand and correct the behavior. Use this approach to show others he learned his lesson."

Fred found and completed an online "Sensitivity in Industry" training course and earned a certificate. He disclosed and owned up to the event when asked about his termination during interviews and then would get immediately right back on point as to how his experience, skill set, and industry connections would best address the hiring company's needs. He had several opportunities with multiple strong job offers to consider in a relatively short period of time. He was employed within two months—even after such a significant, life-changing event!

The moral of the story: Address issues proactively that may surface from a background check. Events from your past that could negatively impact a hiring decision must be evaluated. You must determine how to address them. If they are serious and likely to be disclosed, you may be better off doing so yourself—a better alternative than having a potential new employer uncover the events from a background check. I recommend working with a lawyer who understands the local laws. Validate the best path forward together and consider any fees as a wise investment!

Questions to Be Ready for During a Phone Screen or Interview

Situational and Behavioral Questions

There are several common questions used in interviews. Hiring personnel compare candidates based on answers. "Situational" questions offer insight into how you think you would manage a (hypothetical) work event. These types of questions often begin with "What." For example, "What would you do if you caught an employee sleeping on the job?"

"Behavioral" questions are designed to learn how you handled a real-life situation. An example would be "Tell me about a time when you had to manage a worker who was chronically late to work." The interviewer may ask several questions along a similar line. Discontinuity between your answers is a sign of dishonesty, and answering inconsistently indicates a low degree of skill and competency. Your answers could lead to a bad performance in a stressful work situation. HR folks look for these "red flags."

There is a science behind interview questions. I found a very good article on Indeed.com which is insightful and offers a hiring team's perspective with respect to an interview. The list of questions and explanations that follow provide a glimpse into why these questions are asked, and which character traits, skills, and/or results are being analyzed based on the answers given. I believe these question help you gain a competitive advantage by practicing answering them. Many companies have these common, stock questions on their interviewer forms—and they are all crucial to practice answering! You must prepare for them as practice makes perfect:

1. What career accomplishment makes you most proud?

While it is important to hire someone, who can do the job well, you also want to hire an employee who takes pride in their work. By asking the candidate to share a favorite career accomplishment, you give them the opportunity to share a career highlight—but this will also help you better understand the type of work that makes them feel fulfilled and determine whether it's aligned with what the role entails.

2. Tell me something about yourself that isn't on your resume.

Job-seekers carefully craft their resumes to provide the best summary of their professional experience, but you can't learn everything about a candidate from what they put down on paper. This question is purposefully vague and allows the interviewee to decide whether they want to share something job-related or not. They may choose to tell you about their volunteer work, the sabbatical they took to travel the world, or another defining experience.

The way they choose to respond to this question, and the story they share, can tell you a lot about the type of employee they will be and what they will be able to contribute to your company culture.

3. Why do you want to work here?

This question is your opportunity to determine how much an employee has researched the company, and get a better idea of what they're looking for in an employer. When asking this question, listen carefully for details about your organization and any parallels the applicant is drawing between your company and their career aspirations.

4. What made you want to apply for this position?

This is one of the best interview questions to ask because it delves into specifics about the job role. It shows how carefully the candidate read the job description, and also gives them the chance to share why they'd be a good addition to your team. A well-crafted answer will touch on skills the applicant has as well as skills they want to develop or improve.

5. What are your greatest weaknesses?

This question is one of the most popular interview questions for a reason: it helps you quickly learn a lot about a candidate. This question enables you to deduce three things:

- Whether the candidate's weaknesses could conflict with job requirements or hamper their ability to excel in the role
- Whether or not the candidate is self-aware enough to know their weaknesses without having to think for too long
- How a candidate is working to improve on their shortcomings and have an example of a book you've read, course you've taken, or counseling if required. Definition here will help.

6. What are your greatest strengths?

Like addressing weaknesses, when a candidate talks about their strengths, it shows a level of self-awareness and humility. This interview question also gives the applicant a chance to discuss how their best qualities align with the needs of the role and even demonstrate how they will use their strengths to help the company reach its goals.

7. Tell me about a difficult work situation and how you overcame it.

Everyone has experienced challenging circumstances at work, and often it's in these moments that professionals grow the most. This is one of the best interview questions to ask because it allows the candidate to tell you how they perform under pressure and also discuss their problem-solving skills and ability to manage stress.

8. Why are you leaving your current employer?

When you ask this question, pay close attention to how the candidate talks about their former job. Are they focusing on the negative aspects, or do they err more on the positive side by addressing hopes for the future? The interviewee's ability to show respect for their previous employer and workplace demonstrates their civility and professionalism, which are two essential attributes in any role.

These last two interview questions fit more into the category of "behavioral":

9. Tell me about a time you had to manage a particularly heavy workload. How did you handle it?

This is one of the best questions interviewers should ask because it reveals a candidate's organizational and time management skills, as well as how they deal with stressful situations—such as an increase in workload. Look for specific ways the candidate prioritizes a long list of tasks, adapts to new challenges, and works with others to get the job done.

10. Describe a time when you had to work with someone whose personality or work style was very different from yours.

The ability to work well with other people with different backgrounds, communication styles, and personalities is an important part of nearly every job. This question gives the candidate a chance to show off their teamwork, interpersonal skills, and problem-solving skills, including how they compromise, communicate, and collaborate to achieve a goal or task. It can also give you deeper insight into their personality and work style."

The above list of questions is from an Indeed.com article, "Best Interview Questions to Ask Candidates." I couldn't have a summed up a better list of questions to prepare for.

Phone Screen Follow-Up

After a phone screen, immediately send an email thanking the interviewers for their time. List, using bullets, the top three requirements from the job description and give a brief summary of how you address each. Short and to the point. The "thank you protocol" gets more interesting after an interview.

An example of a phone screen follow-up email:

Subject: Opening #12-E-4487 Accounts Receivable @ Frost Manufacturing—Alpena, MI

Dear Mrs. Rossi:

Thank you for your time today during our phone screen. It was helpful to confirm the top three needs of the job. For your records, here are my qualifications:

• 10 years in accounts receivable	2 roles with 12 and 13 years each
• Track record of lowering DSA	Lowered from >135 to <60 Days of Sales Outstanding
• Flexible 40-hour workweek	Available remotely from 8 AM to 8 PM ET
• 3 Referrals	Former manager and client referrals available

I look forward to hearing from you soon. Thanks again for your time!

Sincerely,

Mrs. Yolanda Smithers

Cell 555-555-1234

YiKES! NUGGET

Personalized, Handwritten Thank You Notes After an Interview

You want to separate yourself from the pack and convince the hiring personnel you are *the* top prospect. For in-person interviews, one effective way is to send a personalized, unique thank you note to each individual you met. You will need to get their business card or contact information. When you arrive, swap your personal card for theirs. Sending a handwritten note of thanks may seem old school and will take some time, but it will clearly get their attention for being unique. Such a note deepens your budding relationship and demonstrates a level of professionalism. Send an email the same day, even if after hours. Then follow up with a handwritten note within twenty-four hours.

I always take the time to send a handwritten note, but in the digital age, an email the evening of the interview or the next day (at the latest) is the bare minimum. Frankly, you should send both for additional reinforcement. Who does this? Those who are the hungriest and want to trigger more discussion and be remembered, that's who! I suggest you carry thank you cards and envelopes with postage on them so you can write a response if you have time afterward. You can do so while waiting for a ride or on the plane ride home, for example.

However, if they are working remotely and you met virtually (i.e., via Teams, Zoom, or WebEx), just send an email. If they are not coming into an office, they may never see snail mail. Consider each situation before acting.

Another communication technique is the "T" letter, described at the end of "Step 2: The Resume." This layout represents the preferred cover letter format; however, it can also provide the structure for a thank you email too. Make it short, crisp, and to the point. Use a bulleted list of the top three to five requirements in one column and list your qualifications next to each.

YiKES! NUGGET

Interview Follow-Up Frequency and Protocol

Regarding when and how to follow up are common questions. In lieu of receiving a rejection call, email, or letter, you will often be left waiting for a response. It is all too common. Therefore, I get asked often by job-seekers, "How and when should I follow up?" I suggest giving them a week. Then, contact the person you most expect to hear from. Get a read on the situation and his/her recommendation.

If you do not make contact, try this. If you interviewed on a Thursday, contact them the following Thursday. If you are told you are on their list, I'd follow up every other week thereafter on the day of the week they advise. If they do not define a day, I'd reach out early in the week on Tuesday morning. Make a phone call. If they do not answer, leave a voicemail—and send an email too.

Call between 7:30 and 8:00 a.m. It is a seller's secret: Folks tend to answer their phone before or after normal business hours. In the morning, people are more fresh and likely to answer. You should also try between noon and 1:00 p.m. or between 5:00 and 6:00 p.m. I know—who leaves voicemail anymore? Professionals do, and in a thoughtful manner.

YiKES! NUGGET

How to Leave a Professional Voicemail

Should you leave a voicemail, make sure to clearly state your name first. Leave a specific and detailed but brief message. End by repeating your name and cell number. Repeat the number a second time slowly as a courtesy. Should they need to jot it down. Be brief and professional and advise that you would appreciate an update on next steps. Advise you will follow up on a future date if you do not hear back from them shortly. Advise them also on the day, date, and time you intend to follow up. Immediately enter a calendar reminder to do so!

Example:

"Hello, Mr. Smith, this is Jack Dempsey. I'm following up on our discussion about the Southeast Regional sales manager position. I believe my thirteen years of developing sellers in the power transmission industry aligns with your need to build a sales force at ABC Company. I'm very interested in joining the team. I'd like to take next steps. If I do not hear back from you soon, I'll try you again next week—Thursday the 23rd at 7:30 a.m. Thanks again! This is Jack Dempsey, and my cell is 555-555-1234. That is 555-555-1234. Thank you!"

Make sure you set a calendar reminder for this exact day and time—and follow through with your follow-up!

Phone Screens and Interviews—Conclusion

Stay positive. Understand that the decision to hire someone can take several months. There are tremendous risks and cost in filling a job. Realize you will not be chosen for the vast majority of opportunities you pursue. Get comfortable hearing, "You are one of two finalists" while knowing you will also hear, "We've decided to go in another direction," or, "Due to economic uncertainty, we are not going to fill the position at this time."

Mike Basmajian, a friend who reviewed Yikes! suggested I address the phenomenon as "Ghosting". This is a frustrating reality in job search. Some folks just completely stop communicating with you or "ghost" you. It's unprofessional, but it happens—a lot. There are many reasons for this, they found another candidate, they decided not to fill the role, etc. It can happen anywhere in the application process and I've even had people say they were ghosted when they expected to get an offer! It's almost incomprehensible, but it happens. It's something that I hope you never experience, but don't be surprised should it happen.

As actresses and actors say, learn to embrace "no." Understand your interviewing skills are improving with each phone screen and interview! The offers will come in time, often concurrently.

There is an axiom regarding how long a job search may take. It states it will take four to six weeks (of search time) for each $10,000 of base salary you seek. In the post-pandemic era, this may grow due to the industry or shorten where there is a rush to hire people back. Today, it is anybody's guess. I'd consider four to six weeks, depending upon the industry and market. Keep perspective.

Wrapping up this section of *Yikes!* has made me think about how job-seekers may be able to overcome any life or career situation through honest, thoughtful, and prayerful self-reflection. You now understand how to address the pain points described in the job description. You can link your experiences, skill set, and tools to convince people you are *the best* candidate for the job!

You need to keep acutely focused on packaging your experiences in a compelling manner. You need to motivate the screener to call you. Then it is your time to shine!

Next, we will discuss how to accept and negotiate a job offer. You will get offers. Chances are, multiple offers!

STEP 5

NEGOTIATING AN OFFER

The goal of every job-seeker is to obtain an offer of employment.

There is an art to how you accept and agree to these terms as this is your one chance to create your compensation foundation with your new employer.

Everything is negotiable; it is a matter of how you ask.

Congratulations, You Got a Job Offer—Fantastic!

You have done it! You've obtained an offer for employment. The number-one objective of every job-seeker, and it's happened! Congratulate yourself and savor the moment! Hopefully, you will receive a second offer that gives you more options and leverage. It is surprising how many times this occurs with mid-career job-seekers. It is commonplace for college graduates too, especially in high-demand industries. Of course, the offer must come in written form—either on a letter on company letterhead or a confirming email from the organization—preferably from their human resources department or hiring manager.

Your initial reaction to a job offer should always be, "Thank you. When do you need my response?"

The offer sets your base compensation. It is the foundation for all subsequent raises and promotions. This will impact your future career earnings. Therefore, it is recommended that you optimize the compensation package. Keep in mind that this will likely not be your last employer. There is nothing wrong with accepting the offer as is. But do not be too quick to accept. And of course, an offer can be rescinded—so be mindful.

YiKES! NUGGET

Do Not Immediately Accept a Job Offer

Ask for some time to "sleep on it."

The biggest thing I've learned in job searching is that an offer is the start of a negotiation. Negotiating an offer is now commonplace. You can always ask for additional compensation, depending upon how good the offer is, to address your personal situation, and/or your desire for the position.

Again, thank the person for making you the offer first. And ask when they need you to commit. They will not expect you to immediately accept an offer and start the following Monday. Well, maybe some will. But that may be a sign that they are a "meat grinder" operation. They bring people on board quickly with a "Let them sink or swim" attitude. This is a situation to be avoided. Some insurance, roof replacement, auto dealers, window replacement, and other business-to-consumer businesses may do this with sellers or technicians. Remember to research and speak with present and past employees!

Companies perpetually struggle to find quality people who fit their team. The number-one problem in small to large companies alike is finding talent. Therefore, there is likely to be some give-and-take when offers are made. Typically, an employer wants to bring an associate on board at the lower end of the compensation scale; however, they need high-quality people. You have some power or leverage in the discussion. Coming in at their level can also slot you for upward promotions in their compensation program, so do not expect to negotiate a 50 percent increase in base pay. Be realistic, but you should ask—as some additional forms of compensation are often available.

The sports "free agent" analogy applies. The better the athlete's skills, the higher the compensation package. You have been selected as the "top pick." Therefore, some aspects of an offer may be negotiated. It is something to flesh out. You do not want to come off as greedy or arrogant. Or worse, act in a way that could cause a retraction. A professional organization will expect you to confirm and validate the offer details. You want to clearly understand them. You now know you are a strong candidate that addresses their needs. You conveyed this during your interview(s). They have confirmed this by making you the offer!

There are variables to discuss, or *negotiate*, when you receive an offer. For those of you who are initially thinking, like selling, that negotiating has negative connotations (taking advantage of another), understand that this is not so. The definition of negotiation is to "obtain or bring about by discussion." This is simply a discussion where you ask questions and gain an understanding. Some of the questions involve the potential for increasing the value of the offer. Think: negotiation and clarification of statements.

Some aspects of an offer are negotiable. Some are not. When it comes to businesses, all have different policies regarding compensation, whether it be a family-run organization, a publicly traded company, or a non-profit 501c3. The flexibility to add value can vary by company. Your research here is key. Family-run organizations might be more flexible regarding increasing employee compensation and/or benefits. Other organizations might provide better benefits such as healthcare contributions or mileage allowance for traveling sellers. Researching and speaking with people who recently worked at the organization is vital.

To give you an example, I helped a nephew, Anthony, negotiate an offer to teach in a private school in his hometown. His first teaching job was in a Southern state. A connection and fellow graduate from his college helped him. He needed to gain experience. Later, with a few years under his belt, he decided that he wanted to move back and be closer to family in Western New York.

Anthony got an offer from a school there. He asked what to do next. He was excited to move close to his family but was unsure whether this would be a good time to ask for something more. We discussed the compensation, benefits, and challenges of the position. He confirmed they needed him, but he had learned they were a privately managed charter school. They had rigid salary structures for specific levels of experience. After a dialogue with a teacher in the organization, in another city, he confirmed he was at the appropriate compensation level. We were confident that salary was not an area to negotiate. However, we knew they wanted him. We also knew there was some leverage, and he should counter the initial offer. We settled on asking for assistance in covering his moving costs. And by simply asking, they agreed to pay $750 to cover a rental truck and travel expenses.

Anthony would have taken the job without the assistance but gained additional value by politely asking. A small win—but a win, nonetheless.

In a personal example, I was promoted to Western regional manager, and we had to relocate from Ohio to Texas. I brought up to my employer a family issue during the discussion of my new responsibilities and compensation. I had to. My wife did not want to make the move. She wanted to stay close to her aging parents—who were presently a five-hour drive away. It would be expensive to fly her back and forth as she was currently making two trips per month to see them and did not want to cut back on her time with them. I mentioned to my employer that she would have to fly and rent a car, which would cost about $750 per round trip, to visit her parents after our move. No sooner did I mention this than my employer offered to pay for one trip per month. I was permitted to have these expenses reimbursed. These terms were added to the promotion agreement by HR. I received additional value just by politely asking.

It is recommended you review the offer and start a discussion. You can make a reasonable request or a counteroffer for something extra. I'd schedule a discussion, preferably in person. For those who have not been in a job search for quite some time, it is acceptable to make a reasonable request for extra value. However, know in advance what you are willing to accept before presenting a "counter." I realize some people are uncomfortable with this approach. This is especially true if he/

she wants the job. That is understandable. But it is highly unlikely an employer would think less of you for politely asking. The worst outcome is being told no. This is just a business decision. So, please consider your options and politely ask.

More Tips Relating to Accepting an Offer

You may want to take a vacation before starting your new job. It is your call. If you are hungry to work, then get on with it. Vacations will come. I've heard of employers frowning on people who say they are enjoying the forced "vacation" of a downsizing. Something to think about. Instead of delaying the start date, you could ask for access to vacation time sooner. Many companies have a one-year eligibility requirement to qualify for ten days (two weeks of paid vacation). So, ask for one week after six months. Or ask for three weeks. Especially if you had three weeks or more in your last job. Have the discussion.

YiKES! NUGGET

Understand Your Budget to Understand Your Compensation Requirements

Searching for work is a good time to review your (family) budget. Determine what you need to live on. This will define your minimum offer requirements. It will also give you a very different task: understanding your budget. Who has the time to do this? You do now!

Like all good financial planners suggest, pay yourself (savings) first every month. Put something into a (Roth) IRA or at least into an emergency ready-cash fund. Even it is only $25, $50, or $100 per pay period. Set the deposit up automatically, then forget about it. Once landed, please start this at once!

If you have access to a 401K, there will probably be a delay of participation for three, six, or more months. However, you can ask to reduce that timeframe. You can also ask for a sign-on bonus to plunk into savings or request that your employer knock down a credit card balance. You just wrapped up a period of time without a steady paycheck, after all, and may have debt to clean up. You can delay the need for an emergency fund. But your first order of business is to account for these monthly necessities:

- Food—groceries
- Food—eating out (which should be minimized when out of work)
- Mortgage or rent
- Car payment
- Emergency fund savings
- Cell phone
- Internet access
- Property taxes
- Homeowner's (or renter's) insurance
- Auto insurance
- Umbrella liability policy
- Utilities: electric, gas, sewer, water, trash
- Retirement savings
- College savings (if yes, start a 529 ASAP! I've not heard of employers contributing to these, but it can't hurt to ask)
- Charitable donations
- Entertainment

It might be a good idea to see where the total compensation package, outlined in the offer, addresses your budgetary needs. Is it at a level you can live on? On the lower or higher end of your budgetary needs? Is there a gap in the benefits you can't live with? Be grateful you have an offer, however, make sure it's acceptable to your needs by doing a budgetary needs analysis and comparison.

YiKES! ASSIGNMENT 14

Define and List Your Budget Elements

Make sure an offer will cover your monthly expenses. However, know the industry, role, and responsibilities. Do the research to understand a regionally competitive salary range and benefits package. The same job will pay differently within forty minutes of New York City versus forty miles from Liberal, Kansas. Also, make sure you understand any city, state income, or other taxes that will impact your take-home pay. Nerd-Wallet has a cost-of-living calculator you can utilize.

I learned about city income tax in Solon, Ohio, the hard way. That 2 percent garnishment was an eye-opener. For those who travel regularly, track your days when you are not working in the city limits because you can file for a city tax refund paid back to you for the days you did not work in town. The prorated portion of the city taxes can be refunded. This is commonplace, and you should investigate it. I sense a niche Yikes! Nugget here. City and regional taxes are becoming more common, and you need to ask about them.

Negotiation Elements

Salary, healthcare, savings contribution (401K match), and any variable pay element, such as a performance bonus or commissions, must be understood. You must grasp what the *net net* will be. This is to know at what level you will walk away. If they are not willing to improve the initial offer, would you accept it? Employers may be able to help, even in some small manner, thereby giving you a better overall compensation package. Remember: They may offer more value for the skills you bring to market.

Some negotiable elements of a job offer:

- Annual salary or hourly rate—define the number of pay periods
- Start date
- Life insurance (often expressed as multiples of base pay)
- 401K program contribution percentage
- Sign-on bonus (tax implications—will they "gross-up" and offset the increased taxes, for example?)
- Company vehicle (model level) or monthly car allowance or per-mile value
- Company-paid travel expense budget or daily "per diem" for room and board
- Relocation expenses to include losses on real estate
- Smartphone included or allowance value
- Internet service and office landline (especially where cell coverage is weak)
- Non-salary compensation—for middle and senior managers or executives (i.e., stock grants or stock awards)
- Draw arrangements—for sellers (i.e., do claw-back terms apply?)
- Paid and non-paid days or weeks of vacation
- Days per week to work from home
- Severance package—yes, you can negotiate a severance or exit plan should things not work out
- COBRA Insurance coverage extension—especially if you have several dependents

A True Story Regarding Benefits

The benefits and the 401K (matching percentage) may be set based on company policy. But it never hurts to ask if they have a greater match available—or if they can shorten the eligibility time. In some unique instances, even publicly traded companies will have different 401K matching percentages for unique circumstances. I was blessed to have an employer double the matching percentage based on the fact that I previously worked there (ten years ago). My match was increased because I had earned a defined pension benefit (during my prior service) that was no longer available. The match was twice the standard percentage. This may be a possibility for you should a similar circumstance exist. More people "boomerang" or return to past employers. Politely asking for a match increase may open a dialogue for some other form of compensation—and all just because you asked! Don't be intimidated or feel bad by asking for something reasonable. If they want you enough to extend an offer, they want you to be happy. And be ready for them to say "no" which is ok too. You're just probing.

Some Observations and Comments Regarding an Offer

Your goal with any opportunity is to get an offer in the form of a letter or confirming email on company letterhead. Handshakes and verbal commitments do not cut it. Get the offer in an email or in the form of a letter. Additionally, it is possible to motivate a company to make you an offer when you make them aware another company is interested in you—if true.

I'm not sure why, other than what I call the "learning-curve effect," but you might be lucky enough to get a second offer shortly after you get the first. This may happen because you have improved your job-searching skills. You have become more self-critical in selecting only solid opportunities, can now package your experiences and skills better, and have become more effective at interviewing. You exude confidence.

When you hear "We will be extending you an offer," you need to think about timing. When you obtain the offer, as indicated earlier, you say, "Thank you. When do you need my response?" They will use your response to gauge your sense of urgency. They may give you twenty-four hours or five business days—or? Offers are timebound. You may want to buy time for other opportunities to mature into offers. You can use the extra time to validate the job is a good fit for your needs and desires. Confirm it is a compensation level that meets your financial obligations. Therefore, unless the opportunity is your "dream job" or you need the job, it is best you buy some time. There will be interest in your skill set and services—and there *always* will be as it is just a matter of timing. A polite way to phrase this is "I'm down another path as far as I am here and would appreciate some time to let it develop." You should let them advise how much time they can extend as it might be more than you think is available. Finally, have the offer letter in hand before you request some time to "sleep on it."

Compensation—Salary or Hourly Wages Can Be Negotiated

I've been a "white-collar" salaried employee since graduating college in the '80s, but the same criteria can apply for "blue-collar" opportunities. You want to be compensated fairly—at average or slightly above average for the position. You do not want to come into an organization at too low a wage. You can use research tools on the web to gain some insights on wages and ask people while networking about wages for different types of jobs.

For hourly employees, a $0.75 per hour increase is significant! A fifty-week year and a forty-hour base workweek is two thousand hours per year. A $0.75 an hour increase (or 50 x 40 x $0.75) will result in $1,500 more compensation in year one! And this will have a multiplier effect with your overtime pay as well...and in future years for setting a higher base.

Department managers and owners of companies will likely advise the going rate for your services. Speaking with people at faith-based job-seeker groups, where HR panels are assembled, is a great way to understand and set your compensation possibilities for specific types of jobs. The North Canton Executive Networking Group now holds Zoom meetings with people participating from around the country.

Ironically, getting paid at too high a level can unrealistically elevate expectations. You can put a bullseye on your back, and if expectations are not met, you will be perceived as an easy way to lower costs in bad economic times. A big salary means big returns will be expected. And rightfully so. I've been in the high expectation "We need a miracle worker" situation before. I was able to deliver on that kind of situation twice, enabling me to get promoted quickly, but also had two instances where expectations were not met. I did not sell enough and was terminated.

In one situation, I was drawn into an opportunity with a very attractive compensation plan. A friend and industry expert waved a bright red flag and said,

"The technology is not ready for prime-time and won't be widely adopted." I took the job anyway and learned firsthand, from clients and prospective customers, the machine (software) was not fully developed and was too difficult to use. My friend was right. After a very difficult year with few "wins," it was easier for the company to get rid of the highly paid salesman (me) than to admit their baby was ugly. In the other situation, the closing rate (for the sale) was much slower than anticipated. In that job, I was told that the prior three reps had all been terminated in two years or less (another red flag I drove through). According to the company, they had not been communicating, documenting their activities (in CRM), or creating a pipeline of opportunities and, in general, were acting autonomously. In that role, I worked numerous ten- to twelve-hour days, communicated with the team routinely, documented call activity in CRM, brought team members on sales calls, and created an $8 million pipeline of potential business. I was terminated anyway—in both instances, after twelve months (one year) on the button. Sadly, I did not see either coming. I was too busy working long hours and addressing the issues they said I should. In reality, I was simply not generating enough sales. A lesson for new business development and sales professionals.

I always put my heart and soul into my work. No one could out-hustle me. Good things tended to happen. However, terminations are decisions made based on business economics. Nothing more, nothing less. They are cold, calculated business decisions. My stories here do, however, reinforce the need for better research of companies and technologies and to network better to understand the circumstances of the position. Networking, listening to, and internalizing valuable input is critical. Not all companies, technologies, and people are created equal. You can learn a lot by making phone calls. Networking (again) is the number-one thing you can do in a job search. It is a critical aspect of your research! *Folks, you need to call and speak with people!*

Non-salary Compensation

For the director or executive (C-suite)-level folks reading this, stock grants or options are potential forms of compensation. The type and amount of those can be highly variable and highly valuable. Your research and discussions with a recruiter, if you are working through one, should address this. Better to get the recruiter's input. The old adage "You do not want to ask a question you do not know the answer to" applies.

Another form of compensation you can ask about when negotiating with privately held companies is ownership in the company, or equity. The nature of your work (i.e., chief financial officer (CFO) or VP of Operations versus a sales representative) will have a lot to do with whether these forms of compensation are an option. Everything is negotiable. This is your one and only time to do so. Using an employment contract lawyer might make sense too.

Networking with people who operate similar types of companies is a wise move when exploring opportunities. SCORE is another potential resource (www.score. org) you can utilize here. Score is an organization that helps people start new businesses and is staffed with volunteers with a wide range of experiences who are committed to helping others. It could not hurt to contact your local SCORE office as they may have people with experiences that can help you understand if your offer is good. Networking is critical in your professional career!

Sign-on Bonus

To my surprise, I discovered that in the mid-2000s, sign-on bonuses were commonplace. They ranged from $5,000 to $10,000 for manager-level opportunities. Senior-level folks were getting stock grants regularly too. I remember a few associates that told me, "I don't care about the base pay—it was all about shares of stock I'd get!" These were surprisingly painless to get. Basically, after you had a written letter extending you employment in hand, regardless of whether you were "at-will" or a "contracted" employee, it was expected that you would ask and likely get additional forms of compensation. Today, the world is a different place, and you may need to be humble based on your industry circumstances. Know the market and what the trends are by participating in job seekers groups—in person or on-line. Or you can be aggressive as so many companies are struggling to find top performers. It is a negotiation!

It is best to do so in an open-ended query versus making a demand (or suggesting a specific value). It is better to say, "I really appreciate this offer and want to join the team. However, is there anything else you can do for my family and me that will help me make this decision easier?" When they say, "What do you mean?" you can respond, "Is an increase in base pay possible?" If the say no, then ask about a sign on bonus. And, of course, enjoy the silence. Let them think about it.

In some instances, folks joining companies in sales will have a modest base salary for six to twelve months to give them time to establish sales that drive commissions. Then the salary ends, and they are paid solely a commission on sales. So, asking for a short-term boost to the base salary, commission schedule, or "draw" is appropriate. Make sure you clearly understand the type of draw and bonus they are offering and consult with their HR representative, with the recruiter, or (if the potential is high enough) with a compensation lawyer. Avoid misunderstandings before they happen.

YiKES! NUGGET

Negotiate an Offer Politely and Smartly

When negotiating additional compensation, do not define it or request a specific monetary value or a specific type of additional compensation. You do not know what they can offer. Simply frame the idea in the context of additional compensation. You can ask "Is a sign-on bonus an option?" But you do not want to say, "Is a $1,000 sign-on bonus an option?" They may have more in their budget (i.e., $5,000), and then you would be leaving money on the table! So, negotiate politely and smartly, and do not use specifics. Ask using open-ended questions, plant seeds of ideas, and then be quiet. See what they can do for you!

Sales Commission Programs

Be wary of salary and draw programs where the draw has a "claw-back" option. I only had this once in my career at a small division of a publicly traded company. Neither I nor my boss fully understood the policy. My compensation had a temporary boost to my base pay for nine months. After nine months, they started reducing my compensation to cover the temporary boost by "clawing back" commission money previously paid. The company thought commissions would have grown to cover this amount as they had a large project they thought would have closed to offset the need to claw back. I even found another large project! Unfortunately, neither closed in the timeframe necessary, and they started taking (clawing) back the prior supplemental salary paid in my first nine months. It was in the fine print of the job offer I just missed.

I was somewhat aware of this clause but never thought it was going to be an issue. They told me the big deal "was in the bag!" I was upset at this. Ultimately, I left because of this issue. Of course, within the following year after I left, both of these deals closed! Live and learn. *Double-yikes!*

I felt awful when I heard that news. However, when I was evaluating leaving that role, I did tell myself (at the time) that if it happened, I would be good with it. And I was. I did fine as I left for another opportunity that had better everything: salary, bonus structure, and company car, and I got a $10,000 sign-on bonus. I still wonder what it would have been like working in a job with unlimited commission potential. An added bonus of the new role was that I met a lot of great associates, many of which who became lifelong friends. Priceless.

Lessons Learned

What this experience taught me was to fully understand the compensation package, especially in sales roles with commissions and the concept of a "clawback, non-recoverable draw"—which is recoverable! I was not fully aware the employer had the right to recover commissions earned to offset the temporary boost in salary. This was on me for not fully understanding how the salary, commission, and draw program worked. Shame on me! And this can happen to you. So, be mindful of the details – and read and clarify the fine print.

Take ownership of the compensation details. If it would help to use a scenario or two, in a discussion with the prospective employer, to gain understanding, do so. Ask people in your network in similar positions about their benefits, commission schedules, or non-monetary perks. You do not want to learn the hard way like I did.

Healthcare, Life Insurance, and 401K Contributions

Benefits, healthcare packages, life insurance, and 401K programs are all unique aspects of your total compensation. Research the local laws to understand the financial impact. Implementation can vary between companies. Large Fortune 500 companies, publicly traded companies, and public sector (schools, utilities, agencies, etc.) employer packages are likely set by HR and non-negotiable. However, you never know what privately held companies can do. You should find out. Approaching this politely and humbly, and in the context of doing the best for your family, provides a platform to ask—and be respected for it. This is just a business decision. There may be a lower family deductible or greater employer contribution percentages or funds dedicated to meet special medical needs. Or a period in which they would pay for COBRA insurance as part of a severance package. Everything is negotiable.

The biggest part about asking is...to ask! Be humble. Use a phrase like "I love the company, the challenges, and believe my skills are spot-on for the requirements of the job. And this is my one and only chance to ask: Is there anything else you can do to help me make the decision to join your team easier?" The trick is to ask the question and then to "be quiet." Enjoy the silence. Hardly anyone asks for such consideration. The person you are asking must take a moment to process the request and think about it. Maybe even jot it down.

The hiring manager or HR representative you are speaking with may be taken aback. Let it soak in. But please, do not feel obligated to immediately describe what *you* want. Do not price yourself out or risk them pulling the offer! Just be professional and polite. They may not be able to do what you specifically ask for; however, if you remain quiet, something good may happen. Be ready to clarify the request should they ask. If they press, be humble and say, "Is extra paid vacation or a sign-on bonus possible?" Always make open ended, non-specific *suggestions*.

For the "Chatty Cathies" out there (like me), just "Shut your pie hole!"

Something good might just come of the request! Heck, it may be a simple gift card with $200 or maybe a $5,000 sign-on bonus or an extra paid day or week of vacation! You just never know.

Company Vehicle, Car Allowance, Smartphone, Landline, and Internet Service

For those of us working in outside sales and/or new business development roles, these are all tools we routinely negotiate or "account for" in the offer letter. However, in the post-pandemic era, with a return to working daily in an office unknown, these remote operating expenses can often be covered by your employer. You will want to have them addressed in the offer letter.

For sellers, Fortune 500 companies are moving away from company vehicles and toward car allowances to mitigate risk and liability. Because of this trend, the base compensation can be increased to offset the cost of a company car. I've always liked having a company-paid-for car or SUV. Primarily, there is no auto insurance exposure when driving it for company business, though you need to make sure how you are covered when *not* on a business trip. Maintenance costs are typically covered by the employer fleet program. With larger companies, there is a pro-rated compensation benefit the company will add to your W-2. This is based on the miles traveled for work versus personal use. You are also limited to what vehicles they have on the fleet "selector."

Some companies have great fleet options while others do not (i.e., an econobox, a premium sedan, an SUV, or a pickup truck). Typically, it depends on the function of the industry/company and your job requirements. The trim level of the fleet vehicles is a function of how much the organization values the role. Service technicians, who live out of work trucks and hotels, are typically assigned high-quality trucks loaded with safety and convenience features. They are considered non-monetary compensation, or "perks." Some companies try to get away with bare-minimum vehicles, affectionately known as "strippers," to keep cost down. Therefore, an allowance may be the way to go. A company vehicle is your (rolling) office, so you might as well enjoy the ride! Ask about the equipment or trim levels of company cars if one is part of the package. Know what you are receiving as part of your package.

I was with a company that employed service technicians who installed complex lubrication systems on customer equipment—often at the customer's facility. The company provided loaded Ford F-250 utility trucks with all the bells and whistles but ironically would not provide uniforms or even disposable Tyvek overalls. Every day, they would get covered from head to toe in dirt, grease, and oil. Because the techs were responsible for their own work clothes, they would often arrive at the customer's shop in nasty, ripped-up, and dirty blue jeans. They often had on filthy T-shirts and ratty ball caps. I was flummoxed, being the guy trying to sell (and cost-justify) our premium systems, since the appearance of these techs did not reflect a world-class organization. If you are considering a job offer that requires uniforms (or should), you should address whether the cost of uniforms will be an expense item. What about laundry service? If required, make sure these are charges you can expense. They may agree to a fixed monthly allowance, and you'll end up ahead of the game—just by politely asking.

YiKES! NUGGET

Account for All Expense Needs in the Offer

If you need a work wardrobe, a specific type of vehicle, or provisions like a laundry allowance, ask about them! Make sure they are included in the offer letter. Just make sure they are reasonable expenses you can have paid for by the employer. Ask and see what they can do!

The caliber of the company vehicle can potentially be negotiated too. I remember renting a van to take a team on a sales call because I did not have a company car. We had the company president along, and I brought up that we rented vehicles for the team a lot. He immediately said, "Well, you are all big guys too [two of us were six feet, four inches], and you should tell Fred the fleet manager that I said for you to order a Dodge Durango [and add it to our fleet]." Granted, I was already on board. But this occurred on one of my early sales calls. It proved to be a testament to "You never know what happens until you ask." Plant the seed.

For most companies, a laptop and a smartphone are standard issue for customer-facing associates. High-speed internet service for your in-home office is also typically an item you can expense. This should be clearly defined in the offer letter. Sometimes there is an allowance. You will want to make sure these meet your budgetary needs based on the cost from the service provider. You should not make money on the deal, but you should not lose money either. An office landline is nice to have but rarely used anymore unless you have poor cell coverage and/or you need it to fax documents. If a fax is required, maybe they can provide a fax-to-computer capability, which many companies need (for example, insurance adjusters, outside sellers, and/or lead-generating service companies). I always thought having a fax-to-computer capability was handy for digitizing photos and documents. This can be achieved with a relatively cheap "all-in-one" office copier today, which the company may agree to buy and maintain (i.e., reimburse you for the toner cartridges). But you will want to confirm such expenses are acceptable and accounted for in the offer letter. Consider the costs if you need to establish a home office, which may include building a room, buying furniture, and getting supplies. When we closed our district offices in the late '90s, we were provided $5,000 to equip our in-home offices.

A video projector for sellers who present on the road is another valuable tool to ask about. This is not a prerequisite as large panel displays are commonplace. But boy, can they come in handy! I love bringing in the projector. On those rare occasions when they are needed, they are perceived as very professional and appreciated by the customers. The show must go on! Your hiring company may say, "Sure, go ahead and expense one when you set up your in-home office!"

Vacation Days or Weeks

A rather innocuous way to get more value in an initial job offer is to ask for more vacation days. I always use this later in the negotiation as a prelude to or as part of a sign-on bonus approach. Generically ask if there is anything else they can offer—and enjoy the silence as they contemplate your idea. If they say, "What do you mean?" You can say, "Extra paid vacation or a sign-on bonus." Depending on how valuable they perceive you and your skill set, and based on their budget, you may get one or both.

Severance

Finally, and slightly ironic, I suggest you ask about severance. What is severance? This is what the company will do should they terminate you—extending benefits or giving you money or supplemental pay for a period of time. Typically, these are done in weeks or months relative to your length of service. They may offer one month's pay for every year of service or one week for every month on a shorter, professional assignment. Or they may have no severance whatsoever.

As an "at-will" employee, there is no reason needed to terminate your employment. You can be told, "It is not working out, and as of today, you are no longer employed here." You may have just experienced this. Frankly, in today's ever-changing and tumultuous economic times, the prospects of getting let go more than once in a career are increasing. Therefore, you should address severance before you accept an offer. It is important to understand whether the employer has a severance program at all. They can leave it out of your offer unless you inquire about it. If you are evaluating multiple offers, severance can be a determining factor.

Given the circumstances, whether you cannot wait to join them or, financially, you need to join them, you cannot ignore the topic. Yet most folks do. However, I believe you owe it to your family and yourself to understand how they treat severance. If they do not have a plan, you can always ask to make something conditional; for example, they could offer COBRA insurance coverage (for some time). If you are lucky, they may agree to do so for three, six, or maybe twelve months. It does not hurt to ask and understand if anything is available. This is especially critical for folks with pre-existing conditions and or a large number of dependents.

There are several approaches to severance. Most companies do not offer anything. Other companies may say there is no severance until you complete one full year of service—then it is one month of salary for every year of service. The more you discuss severance, the more comfortable you will become. It is recommended you first discuss this in a roleplay session with your significant other or a friend. It is a sensitive topic. But you need to put it on the table in the context of a business decision and in "the unlikely event this should be required." Discuss severance as it should be treated like any other benefit. Severance is negotiable. Extending healthcare benefits for your family is a responsible question to ask. Do not suggest a number of months. Requesting "three months of extended COBRA coverage" may cost you an opportunity to receive six months or more. Remember do not give a number first.

It Is Just a Business Decision

Getting let go is the result of a business decision. Addressing severance is therefore appropriate. The stigma of getting laid off, terminated, or fired is not what it was in the past. Getting fired for insubordination or a non-performance-related issue, however, is something you need to correct. Too many really good, high-performing people are let go these days. Companies can impact their bottom line quickly by reducing two things: assets and headcount. They can sell off assets (or not replace inventory) or let people go. It happens all the time. Good people are let go for no reason or because "The business just cannot support the personnel we have," or, "It is just not working out." It has happened to me and is awful. Recovering from such events, and sharing what I learned, motivated me to write *Yikes!*. So, understanding what the company's severance policy is and or defining a severance clause in your letter is an appropriate part of accepting an offer.

Negotiating an Offer—Conclusion

In summary, the goal in a job search is to get an offer! Every time you apply, the goal is to get an offer for every opportunity–you decide to pursue. The big takeaway is that companies are always looking for good people. They strive to get better people on their team. Once you have a written offer in hand, you have some leverage. You can politely exercise it. You owe it to yourself to try.

The number-one issue of any business is finding good people to work for the compensation packages they can afford and have budgeted. Good people with desirable skills can ask for and get extra compensation in many forms simply by asking for it! You owe it to your family and yourself to ask. Now you know how.

YiKES! NUGGET

Ask: "Is There Anything Else You Can Do for Me?"—Then Zip It!

Remember this: Your offer becomes the basis for all future raises and promotions. Be smart about the negotiation and, of course, avoid getting greedy! The best thing to do is to ask, "Is there anything else you can offer to help me make the decision to join your team easier?" Then *enjoy the silence* as they contemplate your question. Let them think about what additional compensation or benefits they may be able to include in their offer.

STEP 6

NETWORKING AND HELPING OTHERS

Thank all your connections who have helped you.

Your networking calls can now change from a request for help to an offer of assistance!

Networking Is *The* Most Important Aspect of Job Search!

Congratulations! You have successfully found a new job! Or you have made a strategic career move to a better opportunity! You endured the marathon of a job search. You may have worked in a bad situation for an extended time and were liberated by landing a new and better opportunity. Maybe you were blessed to be quickly snapped up after a downsizing or layoff. Your confidence is sky-high!

Now is the time to celebrate but not *evaporate!* You need to sustain your new networking habits! Like going to the gym. Set aside time to reach out to friends and associates in your network. Stay connected. Even if you call one person per week, you can become a networking whiz! Use calendar reminders to reserve time to reach out to others – especially strategic connections to include recruiters.

You must stay engaged with folks in your professional life. Even if it is just an occasional phone call or text. You can drop them a handwritten note or a card. Or you can send them a thoughtful gift—especially if they were instrumental in your career advancement. Something personal is best. Perhaps a book or a picture book on a topic they enjoy. There are plenty on sale at your local bookstore. Maybe a link to an interesting article in a text or email. You just never know when these friends and associates will be of assistance again or need *your* help. It is a real possibility that as an "at-will" employee, you may need to touch base again to seek job opportunity assistance. You may need to reload your references, seek a referral, or let them know you are looking—again. Yes, this happens all too often in these times.

I hate to say it, but experience bears this out. Whether you are a recent college graduate or a mid-career reduction-in-force (RIF) casualty, you will likely go through another job search. Even if you roll the dice and become self-employed. You control your destiny when working for yourself, but small businesses are more likely to fail than succeed. Therefore, stay in touch. Stay networked.

As mentioned in the introduction, the number-one thing you can do in a job search is to **speak with people who know you and what you can do!** Talk to folks who know your character. People who understand your successes, areas of responsibility, and your work ethic. People who know what you are good at. Improving the quality of networking calls is one skill you have improved upon during this time, so keep the skill sharp. Have fun networking!

You now know how to leave a brief, on-point voicemail during which you leave your name and cell number at the end. Leaving a professional voicemail message is a good networking habit. Network like a pro! Plant and nurture relationship seeds.

YiKES! NUGGET

Critical Follow-up Items After You Land

Below are three critical things to do after you have landed:

1. Thank *all* the people who helped you! It is imperative that you update them in your network. Do not rely on your LinkedIn profile status change for this. Make it personal. A phone call is the best approach to personalize the message. Avoid voicemail if possible. But after three attempts, you can leave a voicemail (a sample voicemail message follows). A handwritten note is next best, with an email third best—though it is certainly the easiest and most efficient. All are effective and necessary to those who took the time to help. But you need to let your wider network know you have landed. Maybe thank them for their prayers and support if you have that type of relationship. You can never say "please" and "thank you" enough in a lifetime. Reach out to all that helped you no matter how small their effort – especially if they know what you can do!

2. Share your experiences with others who are currently in a job search – offer to help! This is truly the kindest gesture you can make. Offer to assist friends, family, and strangers. Share your stories of frustration, some tips you found helpful, and successes with an empathetic approach. Be supportive of them. There is much you can do to help! Sharing two or three tips can have a profound impact on people who are job-searching. Recommend a book that helped you! A plug here for *60 Seconds & You're HIRED!*, *What Color Is Your Parachute?*, and, of course, *Yikes! I've Got to Get a Job.* Offer ideas. Refer them to recruiters and potential employers. In some instances, just being there and asking someone in the midst of a job search "How is it going?" and then listening to and empathizing with them can mean a lot. As you know, job-searching can have lonely moments.

3. Stay an active networker! During the next four months following your landing, drop a note or call friends in your network to see how they are coping. Have they had any career challenges? Put a calendar reminder out there and follow through. Keeping your network fresh and active is critical. I speak from experience. You can go through a mid-career job search more than once. Stay connected.

While keeping your network alive, it is good to bounce new revenue ideas off people you trust. Ideas for consulting, franchising, and independent contracting (or other income-generating concepts) are becoming more common. You may open doors to new opportunities for yourself as well as those in your network. Pass along opportunities. Suggest that people follow companies you know are healthy and growing. Do this for friends who are presently employed. You never know! Side hustles are becoming more accepted today. The "Gig Economy" or freelancing, outsourcing, 1099 contracting, and other non-traditional "at will" employment opportunities are growing. Some folks suggest employment will shift to more folks working as freelancers than "at will" by 2027.

An interesting phenomenon, when seeking employment as a contractor or freelance agent is to make sure your messaging addresses the client's needs. Your trying to convince them that your services are mission critical to them. Link measurable results, that you're permitted to share and be wise in how you reference past successes as to not share confidential data in your promotional collateral. The use of percentages are best, but try to reference financial impact when you can. Using a phrase like "increased sales >$400,000 (18%) to selected markets for food processing (plastics film) packaging manufacturer, in year one of a marketing campaign" is impactful but presumably vague enough as to not leak confidential data to the marketplace. Be impactful, but be careful not to advise too much information about past clients.

The Power of Working Your Network

A recent company I know well recently had numerous forced retirements and layoffs. One of their top specialists heard I helped folks in their job search. She called me to gauge my willingness to help her. I offered to review her resume and ultimately rewrote it using the four-part layout outlined in this book. Ann was a sales specialist with two fifteen-year-long consecutive series of successes at two different employers: first with an industrial oil seal manufacturer (a seal is a device used adjacent to a bearing to protect it) and then as a sales product specialist selling them. After Ann and I chatted, I referred her to an opportunity in her space at another manufacturer. I made a text connection and got a call back from the sales director (Harriet) on Ann's behalf! She offered two solid leads. First, she told me her company was budget planning for next year, so it was great to learn of Ann's availability. They may have an opportunity in a few months. Second, Harriet knew of a manufacturer's rep firm that might be interested in Ann. One networking connection, in this instance, led to two semi-qualified leads...on behalf of someone else! Both opportunities were only concepts and are only gestating at present, but Ann is now in their line of sight.

These scenarios can and do happen more than you may expect. Companies always have needs and pain points to address but may be waiting for funding (budget) approval. Job search magic. And you too can be a job-search magician!

Back to Networking

Working your network and staying in touch will require you to leave voicemails often. For the record, there are some pointers here. Leaving a professional voicemail will help keep your network vital. The message must be short and positive. If you can lift their spirits when they listen, even better. Here's an example of such a message:

Hello, Frederic! This is Juan Milano. I just wanted to thank you again for your assistance in my job search. I know you probably did not think you helped much, but your ideas and heartfelt support meant a lot to me. Your support gave me confidence that I'd be working again—and I am!

I've landed at ABC Corporation as their manager of Online Customer Service! I've been with them a little over a month. They appear to value my input and are drawing on my experiences. I'm grateful for the opportunity!

How are you? Is everything good at work? I'm here to share my experience in my job search should you ever need assistance. Thanks again for your support! My cell number is 999-123-4567. That's 999-123-4567. Feel free to call me anytime – this is Juan Milano – cheers!"

Helping Others

I can honestly say I derive the most life-fulfilling satisfaction from helping others in their job search. When I'm engaged with a fellow human being at this most critical time after losing their job, it becomes spiritual. I feel most fulfilled. I'm grateful for being able to help them and their family. Being an empathetic ear as they discuss the pressure, they may be under to put food on the table, provide healthcare, and pay the bills is therapeutic. Letting them know you understand what they're experiencing is helpful—for both parties.

I wrote *Yikes!* to give job-seekers peace of mind. Following the **6-Step Process**, you now know, provides you with steps to manage an efficient and effective search. There is a lot of comfort in having a process to follow. Many flounder and think "Poor pitiful me" or "Why me? Now what?" or "What should I do first?"

I know I'm in a better frame of mind and in a great place physically, mentally, and spiritually when I'm engaged in helping a fellow human being in such a difficult circumstance. I encourage you to try sharing your experiences and "being there" for someone. When you do, please drop me a line and let me know how it goes. You can email me at matt@linearcareersolutions.com. I'll do my best to respond.

Remember: The number-one thing you can do to accelerate your job search is to *speak with people who know you and what you can do!*

Here are some key elements to keep in mind for yourself or for others. For people fresh into a job search or for others struggling possibly for an extended period of time (months or longer), remember:

- If downsized, do not worry—this is just a career bump in the road.
- Getting Downsized or terminated is just a business decision—learn from the experience and move on!
- Use the sports analogy and tell others that you are a "free agent" looking for a new team—we can all relate.

- Awesome, valuable, and productive people are all downsized daily. The 2020 pandemic turned many industries upside down, and sector unemployment shot to record levels—you are not alone.

- If terminated, get a clear understanding of what went wrong. What is needed to address the performance gap? Strive to learn from the experience. Avoid the surprises going forward and take corrective action (i.e., an online or in-person course to address the issue).

- When networking, let them know you are available. Ask them to please keep you in mind and contact you if aware of anyone who may benefit from your skill set.

- When you forward your resume, always send it as a .pdf file, which keeps the document layout neat and orderly. Word docs (.doc, .docx) when opened can appear jumbled, especially on a phone. Remember to advise them to check their spam folder for a first-time email if they did not receive it.

- Ask for the name of a recruiter in your industry or target industry, then contact that recruiter and advise them how you got their name. Expand your network.

Networking can become an exciting payoff at the end of a job search. It involves showing your gratitude to those who helped you. Stay active and engaged and *offer to help others!*

Consider Your Casual Time a Potential Networking Opportunity

There are countless examples of how networking has helped me. Several colorful and interesting exchanges proved quite rewarding. Here are a couple of them:

I "pinged" an old associate on LinkedIn, not even a friend, per se, but someone who knew my career trajectory. I was well-known for prospecting and new business development (NBD). I was gainfully employed when we connected, but I was frustrated. I felt my long-term prospects at my current employer were bleak. It was a smaller company with mediocre benefits, low base pay, and no company car. I was working there because the sellers could make unlimited commissions. Several were quite successful and were making well into six figures.

Within a minute of my "checking-in" message on LinkedIn, Matt D. called. That discussion led to an informational meeting. Then an interview. And, ultimately, I made a career move! I worked at this company on a project for a few years and was then promoted to manage their National Aftermarket Sales team. That promotion was additional to my current responsibilities, though. Ultimately, I got overworked and burned out and left. However, I made four lifelong friends who remain in my prayers and weekly communications years later!

Another neat story involves a former boss. I liked working with Mark, and we were part of a new business development team that built an extensive sales funnel. We worked quite well together. Mark and I stayed in touch over the years—just an occasional networking chat often about his beloved Kansas City Chiefs or my Pittsburgh Steelers.

He was recently terminated. Mark is in his early sixties but still has "fire in the belly" and was looking for work. I'm sure he could have retired. However, through a unique set of connections, it was discovered that his skill set was exactly what another former associate of mine was looking for at his company. I have stayed connected with Sam for over thirty years. I learned he was looking for someone in new business development from the industry Mark and I knew. I connected Mark with Sam. They had several discussions and got very close to a deal. They even discussed a potential offer. However, it was not meant to be. Mark and Sam were appreciative of the connection. It was a great way for Mark to practice telling his story during a few phone screens, which included negotiating potential compensation. Sam learned about the headwinds they would face courtesy of Mark's extensive experience in the space.

Never pass up a reasonably good chance to tell your story during a phone screen or interview. And always work toward getting an offer.

Networking Never Gets Old

Another connection with an old friend and customer led to a nice storyline. I heard through contacts that an Area VP at one of our distributors was downsized;

they had consolidated his area into another one to cut costs. I called Larry to check in after twenty years of no communication and offered my assistance. He was blown away, and more importantly, we reconnected as if we had just spoken last week! As if no time had elapsed, despite the fact that we hadn't exchanged a word in twenty years. Really a neat experience. Two sales guy friends chatting it up about his circumstances. I explained what I was now doing, and we caught up on the family stuff too.

Larry is an awesome collaborator and sales leader. His interpersonal skills are well above average. He has business savvy. He has an "uber-professional" work persona folks enjoy. We worked on his resume, and I helped to "level-set" the expectations of his job search. I reinforced that "this is a marathon, not a sprint."

Larry, though disappointed as to how he was treated, took my advice and began using elements of the **6-Step Process**. I advised him to spend some time thinking about his career direction. What did he want to do? I recommended the books *What Color Is My Parachute?* and *Who Moved My Cheese?* to help him evaluate his skill set and learn about other markets, industries, and career paths. Larry was a senior executive with a great track record.

However, he did one thing that I do not recommend. Larry decided to "take some time off and enjoy the family." He did so between the Thanksgiving and Christmas holidays. He started networking and considering opportunities in the new year. One of the neat things he did was reach out to the president of a company who—get this!—Larry had tried to hire twenty years earlier! Now the shoe was on the other foot! Larry told me that speaking with Jim was (again) like old times. They recalled their interview exchange well from long ago.

Thanks to this networking connection, Larry interviewed and got a job within his legacy industry. He did this after two months of elapsed search time (three months if you include the holiday period after his downsizing). He beat the odds, landing quickly. I attribute this to his networking determination and some luck. Yes, luck can play a role. It is good to be in the right place at the right time. The important thing is to put yourself there *because* of networking!

Larry reached out to people who knew him and what he could do. Such people are critical to your job search. Larry's great reputation in the bearings and power transmission industry was spot-on for a new "Accountable Value

Creation" position—a senior leadership role focused on business process improvement and sales development—at Jim's company. A perfect fit...and great job-search success!

Networking and Helping Others—In Conclusion

Losing your job can be devastating. It is especially hurtful to mid-career people who are blindsided. The gut punch is painful. Anxiety gets high...quick. I hope you find *Yikes!* helpful. I hope to deliver you some peace of mind by providing a proven, linear process to follow. You now know the bases to cover with many Yikes! Nuggets to act on.

Job searching is equally daunting for recent college graduates. There is so much you do not know yet. Fortunately, you now know much, much more about job searching from reading *Yikes!* You will enjoy distinct competitive advantages by following the process.

Many of the better colleges and universities out there have outstanding graduate placement statistics. For parents, this must be considered when you are evaluating where your children *should* go to college—it is a big investment. For those on the cusp of starting your career, in an active job search, you must also network. Speak with your (in-major) professors. Work with your parents, family, and neighbors. Reach out to people you interned with or worked with part-time in the summer. These folks all know you, your character, and what you can do. Let them know you are looking for work. They may not have a job opportunity, but they sure may have a referral or connection. Through research, you may find they know someone at a company you are targeting. It happens.

Make a connection. Ask for help. The next thing you know, your resume is getting into an organization and in front of (the eyeballs of) someone with genuine interest in your skill set! Speak with people who know you and what you are interested in doing.

In conclusion, networking and helping others will better position *you* for future opportunities. Those in their forties and older should gird their loins and brace for it. Remember, they are just business decisions. The fastest ways a company can affect the bottom line are to reduce assets and/or headcount. In slow economic times, companies cut production to limit inventory and reduce the workforce.

You have been blessed. You have a one-in-a-million set of experiences. Your family, life, and work experiences all comprise your career body of work. It is a unique and growing set of skills that has *value*! You have tools in your toolbox people and companies need. You have to align with market needs. Take this time to make sure your skills are sharp. Take a class and get certified to close a gap. Make the investment in "You, Incorporated."

Following the tips and recommendations outlined on how to handle phone screens and job interviews are also great ideas to refine and share. Answering the question asked, offering no additional information, and then enjoying the silence is key. Allowing the interviewer(s) to maintain control is huge. Same thing goes for negotiating the offer. Silence is golden. Do not hesitate to ask for more compensation or additional benefits. Tie it to your family budget. Once you ask, remain silent. Do not ramble on or feel obligated to fill the silence. Allow them to process your request and think of what kinds of ways they can address them. You can ask if there are any other forms of compensation they can include to help you make this decision easier—by doing better for you and your family. This is a genuine approach. Even if they say no, you will sleep better at night knowing you explored all the potential compensation elements.

Now that you've landed, get crackin' on the new job. But do not forget to circle back to your network and thank all of those you communicated with. You may need them again, or better still, they may need your friendship and assistance someday!

The number-one thing you can do is to speak with other people who know you and what you can do! Networking is the exciting payoff at the end of a job search. Show your gratitude to those who helped you along with the sixth and final step in the process: stay active and engaged. Offer to help others.

The "psychic income" you will receive (i.e., you cannot pay the bills with it, but you sure do feel good as a result) by lending a hand and pulling someone up in their job search is very rewarding! It is a good, Christian thing to do!

ＹｉＫＥＳ! ASSIGNMENT 15

Contact Someone You Can Assist in Job Search

Think about someone right now who could benefit from your personal contact and assistance in a job search. Jot down the name or names. Make it a point to call them and see how they are doing. See how their job search is going. Feel free to offer some ideas expressed in this book. Better still, offer to meet with them for a coffee and share what you are doing (at your new place of employment) or what you did in your search. See what you might be able to learn from how they are approaching their search; there are always plenty of tips and ideas to exchange. It is interesting how folks in a job search can help each other. This is especially true of referrals.

I'm confident there is a "God Moment" waiting to happen because of a connection you make while helping someone else!

Keep looking up!

Matt Ostrofsky

MY CAREER STORY

I thought it would be helpful if I share my story and aspects of my career progression in this book. It is an account of my early career and how, upon reflection, it helped me create the **6-Step Process**. My career story started with assessing my interests, passion, and skills. The insights I learned are included in "Step 1: Career and Skills Assessment." Later, I was forced into a job search after twenty-four years of continuous service with one company. I experienced a merger and later an acquisition. My experiences opened my eyes to corporate culture—a topic that I'm still learning about everyday.

My big takeaway in my career was how critical it is to evaluate potential employers and their company *culture*. I was good at getting offers and jobs but not good at evaluating the situations I was getting myself into. Culture and technology both negatively impacted me. This influenced me to coach people to keep searching for really good opportunities versus applying to anything and everything you "think you could do." I may have been too quick to make some of my career changes.

I met Tom, a job seeker who targeted (only) one company to join. His network includes people at this global leader whom he knows well. He will stay put in his current job until the right opportunity to join his target company opens up—unless, of course, he becomes a free agent, which recently happened!

My Early Career Story

My career took off in 1983 when I joined the bearings and power transmission industry. My job was training distributors and end-users in bearings (i.e., anti-friction, rolling element ball, needle, and roller bearings). These are

147

high-precision industrial products used in a myriad of machines that keep factories humming. I graduated from the University of Hartford in West Hartford, Connecticut, and was working as a Production Control and Shipping & Receiving supervisor for a manufacturer of plastic beverage bottles in 1981. We developed the PET (polyethylene terephthalate) two-liter soda bottles, which did not require the (black) plastic cup glued to the bottom. The cup allowed them to stand upright. The technology we developed was a game-changer. It eliminated the cost of the tooling for the cup; the material, the glue, and the machinery to put them together probably lowered the cost by 20 percent or more per bottle. It changed the industry forever! I happened to be a small cog in this development. A mechanic, or grunt, really. I supported the engineers working on the project. But I was still involved nonetheless!

Many jobs are obtained through people you know. When I was a college student, my dad tipped me that the bottle technology center was going to hire twelve mechanics. I was good with hand tools. I learned from my dad while working on cars and projects around our house. He encouraged me to apply. I was fortunate and got hired. I worked a couple of summers in this role. During my senior year in college, they posted some supervisory manufacturing jobs. These jobs were in a manufacturing "start-up" as they wanted to generate some cash flow for the site. The location was solely a Research & Development site until 1982. I landed the Production Control and Shipping & Receiving supervisor job in the newly commissioned production plant located on-site. This was after graduating with a bachelor's of Science in Business Administration & Finance. The managers and engineers at the R&D site knew me from my summer work. I was in the right place at the right time—I caught a break. But I also was able to leverage my work ethic. They knew me, what I could do, and how dedicated I was.

My time as a mechanic was a de facto internship and a real blessing. I graduated in 1981 amid a severe economic downturn. I was quite fortunate to land the Production Control and Shipping & Receiving job, which included benefits via the newly legislated 401K savings program.

I was on the pathway to becoming a production supervisor, then a department manager, and, in time, a plant manager—a common career progression in manufacturing. However, I was dating a girl whose parents believed my interpersonal skills were above average. Her dad suggested I try sales—his career path. I was completely caught off guard. Frankly, I had never considered sales. Who wants to bug people to buy stuff? Selling refrigerators, copiers, cars, or whatever was, in my mind, a hassle. The idea of selling made my skin crawl. Her parents made the point, though, that I could try it and return to manufacturing if I did not like it. Great advice from a neat family.

Their confidence in me was motivating. I inquired about what it was like selling with the various sales representatives who visited with me at the bottle plant. Naturally people-oriented, curious, and open to a conversation (some might even call me "chatty"), I developed personal relationships with some of the sellers.

I met all types. They were selling all kinds of different products and services. Contractors for the HVAC systems, representatives for the cartons (we'd put the bottles in), and trucking company reps. Conveyor manufacturers, stretch-wrapping machines sellers, and electrical contractor representatives all worked with me. Even folks from the bearings and power transmission industry would review specs and quote things to me—which I would often review with the plant buyer and controller. I started asking the sellers why they chose selling as a career. Did they enjoy it? After many discussions, one gentleman described the lifestyle of selling in a manner that I could relate to.

He said, "Every day, you come to this building to solve a myriad of different problems. In sales, you get trained in and become a specialist in products and services that solve specific problems. In sales, *you seek to solve the same problems in different buildings, meeting different people.* You work to solve their problems. You use your expert knowledge to justify your solution. It is not like you force your way into the situation, 'sticking your foot in the door,' so to speak. It is different because prospective customers call for help!"

Later, I learned this is a type of selling called "consultative selling." Companies hire people and put them into training programs. They become "factory-trained experts." He said, "Like working with you here at the plant, I make proposals to solve problems. People naturally accept my proposals or buy from me when my solution is the best overall answer to their problem—both technically and commercially. I build partnerships. In many instances, I become friends with my customers!" I really appreciated his characterization of selling! I liked that approach. I pursued a career in sales. Call it a "God Moment."

An Amazing and True Story

With this new awareness of consultative selling, I contacted a recruiter about making the move into sales. I suggested the ideal path for me would be to enter a company as a product trainer and then move into sales. Training would allow me to learn a product and applications that would prepare me to sell. I later learned this notion is from an old Latin principle, "*Docendo discimus*": By teaching, we learn. Training would well-prepare me to solve problems as a specialist and sell to people in a variety of different buildings!

Additionally, because of my mechanical aptitude and experience, I suggested selling something used in a manufacturing plant. Something technical in nature—mechanical or complex—that would solve a problem in that environment. I still had an aversion to selling copiers, insurance, or cars, though all those products solve problems also. I just could not see myself selling those retail products.

I thought of going into a training role due to my passion for presenting or teaching. When in high school and college, I would go out of my way to bring stuff for speech class. I really tried and applied myself when others felt those classes were easy. But I was compelled to make the presentation fun and informative. I like presenting new ideas to people. I really like to get a laugh as well, for that matter, in conversations. Life should be lived well, and humor helps! Watching people light up when they learned something new was satisfying to me. I understand the draw a teaching career can have for many people heading into college trying to determine a career path. I thought a training role would be a good pathway into a company and later into sales.

When I finished explaining my theory, the recruiter laughed. He said, "The economy is in the tank. [This was 1983.] You are not an engineer. The chances of finding a training job that would lead to a technical sales job are minuscule. You better stay on the manufacturing track." Three months later, he called me with a unique opportunity.

The opportunity was for a Distributor Training School Instructor. It would lead to a technical sales role in two and one-half years. It was like a military assignment. The instructor could not get sick, never miss a day of work, and if those hurdles were not enough, there was a catch. I was intrigued by the precise timeline and the catch. Frankly, I was in shock that we were discussing my vision of a training job that would lead to a sales career!

I asked, "What's the catch?" He said, "There's a lot of travel, about 80 percent." I said, "That's like managing a sales territory. Sellers often spend one day in the office [for paperwork and planning] with four days on the road or 80 percent travel." He said, "No, it's more like you depart January and come back in June and then go back out September and return home in November!" I said, "Really? That's a big commitment."

He elaborated, saying, "You will be trained at the factory for a few months. Then, for six months, you will tour the country in a van and be trained by the outgoing instructor. Then you will become the instructor and travel solo for one and a half years. Finally, you will train your replacement the last six months—two and one-half years, like clockwork. The requirement is that you travel for months on end, living out of a suitcase. Checking in and out of hotels sometimes in a different city each night of a given week. The instructor will either conduct three-day-long training classes for twenty to thirty distributor representatives, or present a one-day, eight-hour-long maintenance seminar designed for seventy-five to one hundred or more end-use customers." I said, "Well, what a big commitment, but it is exactly the vision I had in mind, and I'd like to talk to the company about the position." I interviewed and landed the job!

Upon reflection, it was so natural for me to get this role. I was able to address every need the hiring manager had and was not afraid of the travel commitment. And I had genuine passion for public speaking—a key requirement of the job.

Life on the road in the mid-1980s was fun, and the time flew by. It was exciting to find a copy of the *USA Today* newspaper in a hotel, catch ESPN for sports, or find MTV on the hotel cable system—none of which were a given. To see the USA from the highway, versus flying over and looking down over it, was rewarding. I met many good and interesting people, most notably, the local sellers for my employer. I learned many important selling tips, lots about bearings. But a true skill I mastered was how to clarify what people were saying or what they thought they were saying (active listening). One of the most important lessons I learned was that there are as many effective selling styles as there are sellers! Plus, their styles are all unique—no two are alike. All can be effective. Many times, it seemed like working as the Distributor Training School instructor was like attaining a master's degree in the art and practice of consultative selling.

Life on the road had one huge challenge: getting dates. I was always very honest with the ladies and would say I was just passing through. Some appreciated that; most thought it weird. Unfortunate. I had only two long-term, monogamous relationships before I started traveling. The unique circumstance forced me into the singles scene. I became comfortable approaching girls with more confidence as I adapted to my situation. The travel had an additional benefit. I could visit family and friends around the country. My parents and brother lived in Northern California, my extended family was in Pittsburgh, old neighbors lived in Winston-Salem, North Carolina, and many high school friends were in Downers Grove, Illinois.

The entirety of the experience was one of many "God Moments" in my life! When I truly believed God showed favor upon me. He allowed me to realize what was happening and blessed me with safe travels, a great career opportunity, the ability to make many relationships, and, in general, good fortune! Living out of a suitcase allowed me to save much of my paycheck too.

I completed the assignment and was having so much fun doing it, I considered staying out for another year. But I was told, "It is time to move on into sales and earn your keep!"

I was promoted to Rochester, New York (1987) as a district sales engineer. The training experience proved, as I assumed it would, to be extremely valuable. I held lots of training events and was able to use my application and product knowledge to earn business and strengthen relationships. It helped me sell and grow. I was then promoted to regional distributor account manager in Los Angeles (1990). Then to National Distributor Account Manager in Hartford, Connecticut (1993). My sales career included plenty of entertaining, including customer golf, concerts, and industry conferences. I became very successful working with our distributors. I realized when strong personal relationships and friendships could tip business my way—say, when our price was a little higher than the competition.

While in Hartford, I was able to complete a master's in management degree in 2003. My employer paid for me to attend Rensselaer Polytechnic Institute (RPI) in Hartford, Connecticut. RPI was in Hartford because it was a hotspot for big businesses. United Technologies, Otis Elevator, Carrier, Stanley Works, Aetna Insurance, and numerous other large companies are headquartered there. The RPI program was wonderful as it was taught by many active and retired Coast Guard veterans—a wonderful group of dedicated professionals. Proud Americans. Did you know that the Coast Guard is the only government agency with both policing and military authority? Yes, that was news to me too.

During this time, my employer was acquired by a larger bearing manufacturer. I was happy to learn the acquisition would make the newly joined companies the largest broad line bearing company based in the United States. I thought the glide path into the next phase of my career was all set. I was promoted to world headquarters (Canton, Ohio) in 2004 to manage a six-person team of strategic account managers. We were responsible for our top five distributors, commanding $225 million in sales. I became involved in hiring and training our sales engineer recruits too—the ones who would work with distributors. We would hire them out of college and classroom-train them for eighteen months, and while in the program, I would train them how to sell to and through our industrial distributors.

However, once off the road and in a corporate environment, I realized the culture of the acquiring company was very different. Their philosophy toward distributors was formed by having tremendous market share. They "owned the market" in only one type of bearing. I was brought up in a company with several more commodity-bearing types with much lower share (for each type). So, I now had experience with two very successful organizations with two very different worldviews based on their market position. They also had two very different approaches to selling to distributors. Your world view is quite different when you have 90 percent market share versus 10 to 20 percent. Things in corporate did not go smoothly for me – a clash of cultures.

Basically, it was a tale of two extremely unique corporate cultures, both successful. I had been working for the low-market-share company. We were nimble, customer-service oriented, aggressive in marketing, and hungry for sales. The company that acquired us was the proverbial "eight-hundred-pound gorilla". It had a high market share and operated slower and more conservatively with a "take it or leave it" attitude. Because it could. Leadership had no interest in understanding what worked and how we sold our broad line, our brands, etc. They even decided to drop a key brand and an iconic logo that was very much part of our story. My time in the corporate office wore me out. So, while gainfully employed, I began to seek other opportunities. I was open to a different industry and was determined to get back to my true passion: customer-facing, field-based, consultative selling.

The move from field sales into a corporate position helped me learn where I would be the happiest. For me, that is in customer-facing sales. It is what I love to do. Where I generate unique and greater value by developing personal relationships with customers, which drives new business. Frankly, I have more fun in sales. My curiosity grew in seeing how transferrable my selling skills might be in another industry. So, off I went to search for another industry with a new company, new products, and a new culture.

I was able to make a move in several months. Through a friend, someone who knew me and what I could do, I was able to land a great opportunity selling physical security products, specifically, electronic door hardware. An important lesson to note: This opportunity came about through networking. *The number-one thing to do in a job search!*

Because my friend had opened the door for me, it was relatively easy for me. I still had to sell myself, however. And I had to prove that I met their requirements and fit the culture. My friend helped me prepare for the interviews, providing insight on the products, competitors, issues, and most importantly, who I would meet for the interviews. I was well-prepared. I cannot say I had it in the bag. But I knew that if I did not blow the interview, I would get the job. The compensation package was a tick better than what I had, and it included a company car, so off I went.

I sold electronic locks and software into the kindergarten to high school (K-12) and higher education markets. It was an exciting and growing field with plenty of schools getting retrofitted or constructed. Demand was high. I soon realized my professional selling and interpersonal skills were transferrable. In two years, I was fortunate to be part of a team that landed the largest order (as measured by the number of electronic locks ever sold) to one site! I was then able to set the stage for the next big order in the industry. I figured I was well on my way in my new job and would retire with this company. A reduction-in-force (RIF) downsizing was the last thing on my mind.

In April 2010, after the company had two layoffs in 2009 (thanks to the 2008 mortgage default swap and real estate crash), my job was eliminated.

I was crushed. I had not been out of a job since my dad taught me how to cut the lawn when I was nine years old. That was one of my chores, with a walk-behind power mower that did not have the blade-release clutching system (for safety) they have today. Yikes!

My reduction occurred as the effects of financial meltdown swept through the economy. As the sole provider, I had the full suite of life's responsibilities on my shoulders: a wife, a child, a mortgage, utilities, health and life insurance, a car loan, a cell phone plan, an internet cable subscription, and college savings obligations—along with two cats to feed. The pressure to get a positive cash flow situation was huge. When you stop and realize all these burdens are on one's back, the pressure becomes intense quickly! I was shell-shocked. I only took one day to mourn, though. The next day, I was back on the horse, looking for a job. My new, full-time job.

For several years, I had always helped people write or improve their resumes. It was a hobby. Now, however, I was tasked with updating mine while under pressure. Stressful for sure. Time to put one foot in front of the other. I updated my resume and began a search.

Some Perspective—Why the 6-Step Process Works

I felt I had a pretty good grasp of what it would take to sell myself and find a new job. I was searching after the downsizing in 2010 ("job eliminated due to the 2008 economic downturn"). But honestly, I had only searched one other time—when I was employed. I had not been under the gun to make a move then. I had been secure with a paycheck.

My search after the downsizing was different, more intense, more urgent. Then another "God Moment" occurred. I was introduced to the North Canton Executive Networking Group (NC ENG). Susan Shearer, a former associate, heard I was looking for work. She mentioned the group. The positive experience I had working with the volunteers at NC ENG triggered my interest in framing job search as a process. This is where the idea about a book started so I could help a broader audience.

It is funny in a way. I enjoy selling so much, I've kept myself in a customer-facing or prospecting role for most of my career. I was promoted into a corporate role but found it was not as fulfilling or as fun as field sales. I ultimately got back to selling, where I remain today. Working hard at developing relationships, listening to customers' needs, and determining how to best solve them. In some instances, we recommend a solution we do not offer by pointing out a competitor's solution—always trying to help the customer. Always trying to do what is right.

My career track remains satisfying. It has enabled me to provide for our family while allowing me to follow my passion of helping others in their job search and to write *Yikes!* Ironically, the devastating 2020 pandemic helped. Due to furloughs, I was afforded the time to draft the manuscript. None of this could have happened without the support, love, and dedication of my beautiful wife Andrea. She is smarter than me and helped develop *Yikes!* Two true "God Moments"—meeting and marrying her!

I hope you found my story and passion for helping others inspirational. It is my strong belief that you, too, will learn much in the science of the job search. Mastering the **6-Step Process** will help you now and very likely in the future. Once you land, please thank those who have worked on your behalf. No matter how slight their support was, thank them all. This is nurturing your network.

Finally, I hope you take the time to help others in their job search. I believe you will find that highly rewarding. Thank you for reading the book and all the best in your job search – I know there are many tips you can benefit from and I hope you start the process now!

ABOUT THE AUTHOR

Matt Ostrofsky is a successful technical seller, consultant and trainer who solves complex commercial and mechanical system problems. He has a zeal for life and a spontaneous sense of humor he attributes to his family moving often when he was a child, so he had to learn how to break into new environments and work with strangers. At 6'4", Matt stands out in a crowd. Most importantly, he has a deep passion to help others.

After graduating from the University of Hartford with a Bachelor of Science in economics and finance, he began working as a production control & shift supervisor in manufacturing. He realized he enjoyed working with the salespeople who visited him. This opened his eyes to a career in sales and he secured an opportunity to learn a product (bearings) through training. After three years of touring the U.S. as a public speaker, he was promoted into sales. Matt furthered his education at Rensselaer Polytechnic, earning a Master's degree in management which emphasized accepting new technology, driving innovation, and how everything comes down to organization behavior and interpersonal relationships—all relevant when searching for a job.

Through the years Matt has focused his leisure time to helping others in their job search. After he experienced a downsizing, he became affiliated with volunteer job search support groups and volunteered with the North Canton Executive Networking Group in North Canton, Ohio. He realized there are many aspects to executing a job search. He learned the job search process through trial and error and how the coaching provided by the volunteers was helpful. He also witnessed how people flail, fail, and get frustrated and anxious due to the steep learning curve of job search.

Matt saw a need for bringing order to the initial chaos of a job search. An ordered or linear process to a job search was needed. This prompted him to create *Yikes! I've Got to Get a Job.* Yikes! offers a 6-Step Process for getting ready, managing, and completing an efficient job search. Additionally, it prepares readers for the onboarding process after landing a new job.

Matt leads a suburban life with his family in Georgia. He and his wife volunteer and have never binge watched a cable series, though they enjoy relaxing at the movies. Matt has volunteered in many areas, softball coaching, home owners associations, community groups over the years. While preparing to publish this book, his full-time sales role and the book launch have been his top priorities. He considers housework and chores like cutting the lawn hobbies and a means to stay healthy. Once in retirement, he looks forward to providing job search consultations and teaching the *Yikes!* 6-Step process online and in person.

To learn more or contact Matt, visit www.YikesIveGottoGetaJob.com.

ACKNOWLEDGMENTS

I'd like to acknowledge the various people who helped me develop this concept into a book.

- **Andrea Wander**—my loving wife and one of the smartest people I know
- **Matt and Lucille**—my parents who instilled a work ethic in me that keeps me motivated at work and in my volunteering
- **Mike Basmajian**—longtime friend and business associate who critiqued Yikes! and shared how the "one-pager", marketing brief helped him tremendously
- **David Burns**—former manager, chemist, Christian, and friend who was "retired" before his time and had a successful run in franchising after his corporate career
- **Michael Coyle**—author and technical guide to writing and publishing who recently passed away
- **John DiNallo**—longtime recruiter who provided inspiration and insights and with whom I have an ongoing friendship
- **Dr. David Hammond and Jim Donavon**—inspirational pastors who helped frame the introduction, with David suggested to make it a "workbook" and Jim inspired the be grateful section
- **Pat Fladung**—NC ENG volunteer, neighbor, and the most passionate and knowledgeable person I know with respect to job searching
- **Ralph Hansen**—a friend who gave me some insights as he was in a job search during the early days of this writing

- **Andy Geremia**—longtime associate/friend last minute key contributor with respect to some context and formatting
- **Lori Hiett**—friend and associate who provided specific insights and early observations of the draft—emphasizing the female point of view
- **Jamie H. Martin III**—former manager, mentor, longtime friend, and the most business-savvy guy I know
- **Mark Morek**—recruiter and longtime friend who brought much-needed depth and industry perspective that softened some of my views with alternate ideas
- **Chris Mosby**—longtime associate and Christian friend who made the point "Your story is important, but get to how the book can help the reader quicker," so I reordered things
- **Scott Prescott**—longtime professional consultative seller, investor, cyclist, and dear friend and moral supporter
- **Andy Reichlin**—work associate, longtime friend, English major, and wannabe author who has a great sense of humor and who edited the manuscript, taking rough edges and many grammatical issues off the table
- **Jeff Stoller**—a retired associate from the bearings industry who recently "boomeranged" back to our longtime industry and provided insight
- **John Zanath**—another longtime friend and deep thinker who edited and critiqued Yikes!
- **Harry and Rita Zander**—who encouraged me to pursue a career in sales

REFERENCE

Yikes! Nuggets and Assignments—Cross-Reference

This section lists the Yikes! Nuggets and Assignments

Introduction to the 6-Step Process

- Yikes! Nugget: Invest in Your IT Infrastructure (page xii)

  - Buy a new laptop with Microsoft Office Word, Excel, and Power-Point installed
  - Get a secure Virtual Private Network (VPN) for security
  - You will need this for resume writing and PPT should you be asked to present on an interview

- Yikes! Nugget: Use a Personalized Voicemail Greeting (page xiv)

  - This will give you a sense of the flow of the process
  - It will allow you to implement some of the Nuggets immediately

- Yikes! Assignment 1: Define Your Core Values (page xix)

  - A critical thinking exercise about what drives and defines you!
  - List at least four Core Values

- Yikes! Assignment 2: Write Down 10 Things You Are Grateful For (page xxi)

- An endorphin-releasing exercise to help you keep perspective
- This will help you keep a positive attitude during what might be a long journey

- Yikes! Nugget: Call and Speak with People Who Know What You Can Do (page xxii)

  - The number-one thing you can do to help your job search!
  - Challenging at first; by the end of the process, you will be a helpful resource to others

Step 1 | Career and Skills Assessment

- Yikes! Nugget: Great Reference Book: What Color Is Your Parachute? (page 4)

  - Use it to support your career assessment

- Yikes! Nugget: Critically Evaluate Your Fit to the Job Description (page 6)
- Yikes! Assignment 3: List Your Experiences, Competencies, and Skills (page 8)

  - List at least four each

- Yikes! Nugget: Keep a Notepad and Pen on Your Nightstand (page 11)

  - Many people have great recollections in the quiet times before they fall asleep, or they wake up with great ideas
  - This will allow you to capture a note and allow you to return to sleep

- Yikes! Nugget: Develop a Thirty-Second "Elevator Speech" (page 21)

  - A crystallization of what you do
  - Necessary for introductions when networking

Step 2 | The Resume

- Yikes! Nugget—Include a Compelling Professional Summary (page 25)

- Capture the essence of your career and aspects that are uniquely you
- Custom-tailor this to each job you apply to
- Use a phrase that is memorable to hook the reader to you

- Yikes! Nugget: Yikes! Nugget: The Four-Part Resume Structure: For the Experienced Professional (page 25)

  - Professional Summary
  - Competencies
  - Experience
  - Education

- Yikes! Nugget: The Four-Part Resume Structure—College Graduate (page 26)

  - Education
  - Experience
  - Skills and Competencies
  - Involvement

- Yikes! Assignment 4: Start Your Resume with Contact Information (page 27)

  - Do not use your full street address; rather, only a (metro) location
  - Cell number, email, and hyperlink to your LinkedIn profile

- Yikes! Nugget: Get a Modern Email Address Domain (page 28)

  - Using "Joe.Blow@aol.com" indicates you are old

- Yikes! Nugget: Always use a keyword match to optimize your resume (page 34)
- Yikes! Nugget: Font size and type (page 29)
- Yikes! Nugget: How to Treat Acronyms (page 35)

  - Spell the phrase out, followed by the acronym in parentheses
  - Return on Investment (ROI)

- Yikes! Assignment 5: Add Your Professional Summary and Competencies Table (page 37)

  - As you build your resume, you will want to add these sections one at a time
  - If you use MS Word, do not use the resume formatting tool as it becomes too difficult to manage when customizing

- Yikes! Nugget: Use Numbers, Dollars, and Percentages to Define Your Impact (page 39)

  - Defining the impact of your work will separate you from the pack
  - Using numbers and percentages will give you a competitive advantage

- Yikes! Nugget: Resume Guidelines, Dos, and Don'ts (page 41)

  - This list is a great reference. You never use the word "I" on a resume
  - Do not use an "Objective Statement" or "References Available Upon Request"

- Yikes! Assignment 6: Develop a SOAR Story (page 43)

  - Describe a success you created or were part of
  - Use numbers, dollars, and percentages to show impact
  - Do not worry about the size of the impact; the method and story are the message

- Yikes! Nugget: Proper Formatting of Job Duration (page 44)

  - Critical for ATS filtering; use a two-digit month, then a hyphen, and then a four-digit year
  - Consider using only a four-digit year (no month) for choppy careers with multiple jobs per year
  - A marketing brief may be a better option

- Yikes! Nugget: College Internships Are a Great Career and Networking Launching Pad (page 48)

- · The job placement rate for college graduates is a good metric to understand

- Yikes! Nugget: No Typographical or Grammatical Errors Allowed (page 49)

  - · Applicant Tracking Software (ATS) has the ability to pass over resumes with errors
  - · Double-check that your title sections are spelled correctly as MS Word can miss title errors
  - · Internships are an invaluable way to get a jump-start on your career and network

- Yikes! Nugget: Describe Currency Consistently (page 54)

  - · Use "K" for thousands, "M" for millions, and "B" for billions with a currency symbol
  - · Examples: $450K in Sales, $2.5M in Revenue, and $65B Division of ABC Corporation

- Yikes! Assignment 7: Add Your Experience Section (page 55)

  - · One-sentence brief description
  - · Bullets of responsibilities with quantified results
  - · Give size and scale and show impact

- Yikes! Assignment 8: Add Your Education Section (page 57)

  - · Do not show years graduated
  - · List grade point average only if stellar: 4.89 (5.0 max) GPA

- Yikes! Nugget: Create and order your personal business cards—now! (page 61)
- Yikes! Nugget: Create Your Cell Phone vCard (page 62)

  - · An electronic contact card of your information for ease of sharing
  - · Do not include your complete home address

- Yikes! Nugget: Create and Manage Your Reference List (page 63)

- Contact and ask their permission
- Have them reinforce a skill important to the hiring team

- Yikes! Assignment 9: Create Your Reference List (page 64)

  - Have three personal and three professional references

- Yikes! Nugget: Contact All Parties on a Reference Request Via Email (page 65)

  - Make sure you tip your references that they will be contacted

- Yikes! Nugget: Organize Your Hard Drive (page 65)

  - File searches by company and position

- Yikes! Nugget: Update Your Resume Annually (page 66)

  - Do this in preparation for your annual performance review

Step 3 | LinkedIn and Applying Online

- Yikes! Assignment 10: Create or Update Your LinkedIn Profile—If You Need One (page 72)

  - LinkedIn is the top database people use to search for talent—whether you like social media or not
  - Dress up and have a professional portrait photo taken—this service is often free at job search groups

- Yikes! Nugget: How to Request a Recommendation on LinkedIn (page 73)

  - Do not give someone an assignment—make it easy for them to recommend you
  - Draft the Recommendation for them and ask them to edit and approve
  - You control whether to post it

- Yikes! Assignment 11: Research a Company Where You Will be Interviewed (page 77)

  · Research their financials and the governmental and environmental issues impacting them
  · Research people you will be interviewing with
  · Speak with past employees to gain some perspective
  · Understand how the position impacts their mission

- Yikes! Nugget: Avoid the "Time-Trap" of Blindly Applying Online (page 80)

  · Applying online can be a distraction
  · Focus more time searching for better opportunities and networking

- Yikes! Nugget: How to List Salary Requirements When Requested While Applying Online (page 81)

  · Avoid answering if the system permits you to leave the field blank or use $0
  · Respond with "Market Competitive" if the software permits text
  · If a numerical value is required, use your research and budget requirements and insert a market based value, don't wing it or shoot ludicrously high

Step 4 | Phone Screens and Interviews

- Yikes! Nugget: Plan to Interview the Company (page 87)

  · These are two-way discussions where you want to address their needs first
  · You want to learn about how they treat associates and learn about the culture

- Yikes! Assignment 12: Create Your Interview Questions (page 87)

  · Inquire about issues you learned from research
  · Ask open-ended questions: "How do they treat people?" "How

would they describe the culture?" "Would you recommend family to work here?"

- Yikes! Nugget—Answer the Question Asked and Address the Needs Listed in the Job Description (page 88)

  · Keep in mind they have needs expressed in the job description
  · Reinforce how your experience, skills, and interests address their needs

- Yikes! Assignment 13: Practice an Interview (page 91)

  · Practice interviewing with a spouse, friend, or a job-seeker buddy
  · Work on answering the question asked and do not offer additional info
  · Let the interviewer maintain control

- Yikes! Nugget: First Impressions Matter and Execution Tips (page 93)

  · Dress appropriately given the company culture—if unknown, suit and tie
  · Make eye contact and repeat their names back
  · Have excellent posture

- Yikes! Nugget: Send Personalized, Handwritten Thank You Notes After an Interview (page 108)

  · Separate yourself from the pack
  · Get an appropriate snail-mail address during the interview and send a note of gratitude
  · Make sure they will be at that address (their office or home address)

- Yikes! Nugget: Interview Follow-Up Frequency and Protocol (page 109)

  · Set calendar reminders and follow up

- Yikes! Nugget: How to Leave a Professional Voicemail (page 110)

  · Introduce yourself, be brief, and be professional
  · State why you are a strong fit and are interested in joining the team
  · State your name again and leave your cell number—slowly repeat it a second time

Step 5 | Negotiating a Job Offer

- Yikes! Nugget: Do Not Immediately Accept a Job Offer (page 114)

  · This is counterintuitive, but this is an emotion-driven sequence
  · Say "Thank you," and ask, "When do you need my response?"
  · You want some time to digest, form clarifying questions, and let other opportunities come to conclusion
  · Second offers are often realized as you have leverage with an offer in hand

- Yikes! Nugget: Understand Your Budget to Understand Your Compensation Requirements (page 117)

  · List and total the value
  · Include some value for your savings—your first monthly expense

- Yikes! Assignment 14: Define and List Your Budget Elements (page 119)

  · A must-review to ensure you negotiate an offer that meets your needs

- Yikes! Nugget: Negotiate an Offer Politely and Smartly (page 125)

  · Consider the many compensation and benefit elements to negotiate
  · Even address severance as a negotiation element

- Yikes! Nugget: Account for All Expense Needs in the Offer (page 129)
- Yikes! Nugget: Ask: "Is there Anything Else You Can Do for Me?"—Then Zip It (page 133)

  · This is a safe, innocuous way to see if the offer can be enhanced
  · Ask the question and remain silent—there may be a long, pregnant pause

Step 6 | Networking and Helping Others

- Yikes! Nugget: Critical Follow-Up Items After You Land (page 137)

  · Thank all who helped you
  · Share your experiences with others who helped or need help
  · Stay an active networker—methodically plan follow-up contacts

- Yikes! Assignment 15: Contact Someone You Can Assist in Their Job Search (page 146)

  · This will keep your skills sharp and your network fresh and active
  · Helping your fellow man can be very satisfying

How-to Suggestions

How to insert a hyperlink (into your LinkedIn profile):
https://www.youtube.com/watch?v=EgmU6OcYC9U

How to create a basic Return on Investment:

https://www.business.org/finance/investing/
how-to-calculate-return-on-investment/

Reference Websites

Healthcare

https://www.healthcare.gov/

https://www.kff.org/interactive/subsidy-calculator/

Job search groups and assistance sites:

https://nceng.weebly.com

http://www.careerladders.com

Research Websites

For information on companies: Search the "News" section of company websites

www.hoovers.com

www.dnb.com

DISC personality test:

https://www.123test.com/disc-personality-test

Keyword match website:

www.resunate.com

www.skillsyncer.com

www.visualCV.com

www.vmock.com

www.jobscan.com

www.rezscore.com

Job listing portals and research (available as smartphone applications too):

www.indeed.com

www.glassdoor.com

www.ziprecruiter.com

www.acquirent.com/sales

www.resumelibrary.com

www.fairygodboss.com (women focused)

www.idealist.com

www.lawjobs.com

www.hired.com

www.mediabistro.com

www.recruiter.com

www.usajobs.gov (government jobs)

www.recruitmilitary.com (for veterans)

Aerospace industry jobs:

https://aerospace.org/careers

Computer, Programming, and IT industry jobs:

www.dice.com

How to evaluate if a franchise might be right for you:

Why Franchise? Evaluation Process
Forbes 2018 Article "How To Know If A Franchise Is Right For You?"

Resume writing services

Top Resume Writing Services - Atlanta
https://zety.com/blog/resume-writing-services

Social media profile cleansing

https://www.scrubber.social

[QR code]

https://www.businessinsider.com/
scrub-social-media-delete-job-application-2019-9

Career Direction Change—Evaluation Resources

https://www.businessinsider.com/
scrub-social-media-delete-job-application-2019-9

[QR code]

www.reputationdefender.com

[QR code]

College students who need their social media profile sanitized:

https://www.scrubber.social

[QR code]

Sources for Business Cards

FedEx Office www.fedexoffice.com

[QR code]

Vista Print www.vistaprint.com

[QR code]

Overnight Prints www.overnightprints.com

[QR code]

Blockbuster Print www.blockbusterprint.com

Interview Dress Recommendations

This "Dress for Success" Facebook site has current trends and tasteful suggestions (note: this may be a women's group):

https://www.facebook.com/DressForSuccess

Drug Screen References

https://www.drugs.com/article/drug-testing.html

https://my.clevelandclinic.org/health/diagnostics/10285-drug-testing

https://nida.nih.gov/nidamed-medical-health-professionals/
screening-tools-resources/chart-screening-tools

Med Access Guide to Drug Testing

https://www.medaccess-uc.com/employers/services/drug-screening

Cost of Living Comparisons

https://www.nerdwallet.com/cost-of-living-calculator

https://smartasset.com/mortgage/cost-of-living-calculator

https://www.payscale.com/cost-of-living-calculator

Recommended Books

- *What Color Is Your Parachute?* (**Current Edition**)

Author: Richard N. Bolles
This is a fantastic self-help book with a variety of self-assessment and self-interest tools to help you focus your search in areas you are interested in and qualified to explore. It evaluates market phenomena and industries for growth potential. This book is updated annually, so always get the latest year available (i.e., 2021, 2022).

- *60 Seconds & You're Hired*

Author: Robin Ryan
This is an invaluable book on the job search process with exceptional guidance on how to handle phone screens and interviews. I wish I had read this before my infamous interview at the truck parts manufacturer in Texas.

- *Who Moved My Cheese?*

Author: Spencer Johnson, M.D.
A quick read that most can finish in under an hour. It is a parable with plenty of insights designed to help readers manage and cope in turbulent and changing times—a timeless book, given the impact of the pandemic on the world economy. Written for all ages, it is a story with insights that can help people throughout the course of their career and into retirement.

APPENDIX

Reference Resumes and Documents

Recommended Resume Formats:

- Format for blue or white collar professionals with up to 35 years of experience (keep to 3 pages and 2 is best if possible):
  - Professional Summary
  - Competencies (an optional table of 9 key words or phrases)
  - Experience
  - Education & Certifications

- Format for people with skills marketed to the "gig marketplace" or with greater than 35 years of experience - the one page "marketing or networking brief"
  - Descriptive Career Banner (one line)
  - Recent Experience
  - Creates Value By
  - Target Company Strategies
  - Areas of Expertise
  - Target Company Markets Served

- Format for recent college graduates:
  - Education
  - Experience
  - Skills or Skills and Competencies
  - Involvement

Samuel Shelby - Resume Before Yikes!

SAM SHELBY – BEFORE YIKES! RESUME

1234 street address * City, State 55455 * Mobile# 999-999-9999 * email: samtravelerman128@aol.com
LinkedIn Profile · Twitter/Blog/Portfolio

EXPERIENCE

JULY 2017- DECEMBER 2018

ABC
Territory Manager Southwest Region

*Responsible for East Texas, Louisiana, and Arkansas areas. 6-7 million dollar territory
*Proactively worked with distributors within the territory. Distributors include ABC Industries, Chaps Industrial Technologies, F411 Bearings & PT, and Ned's
*Major end users worked with included International Paper, Georgia Pacific, Tyson Foods, Graphic Packaging, Benteler Steel, Pilgrim's Pride and Norbord
*Prospecting for new customers
*Provided product training for distributors and end users

APRIL 1993- JUNE 2017

FREDS INDUSTRIAL SUPERMART
General Manager, Waco, Texas Service Center, May 2007- June 2017

*Maintained and communicated corporate strategies to the Lufkin service center
*Coordinated efforts internally with sales and corporate marketing team to meet sales and placement goals
*Proactively engaged in high-level dialog with purchasing and maintenance teams to clearly understand customer's needs
*Created store budget for service center each year. 4-5 million dollar budget
*Created continuous learning programs for each employee of the Lufkin service center
*Closely monitored training programs to make sure each employee was on pace
*Industries serviced in the Lufkin area included pulp and paper, lumber, food, aggregate, and printing

Outside Sales Representative , May 1997-April 2007

*Built strong working relationships with the national account customer base. Customers include Georgia Pacific, International Paper, Champion Paper, Tyson Foods, and Pilgrim's Pride
*Responsible for growing business with small and medium accounts
*Worked to maintain, cultivate and manage business relationships within each account
*Responsible for weekly reporting of all end-user calls including successes and lost sales

Customer Sales and Service Representative, April 1993- April 1997
*Worked closely on the phone with customers daily to fill orders and help solve customer problems
*Built strong relationships with customers by taking care of all daily needs in a timely fashion.
*In charge of weekly customer order follow up calls
* In charge of all back order reports

EDUCATION

AUGUST 1972-AUGUST 1974
Texas A & M – College Station, TX
- o   Business Administration
- o   Dean's List

SKILLS

- Software Proficiency
  CRM, Microsoft Outlook, SAP

Samuel Shelby - Resume after Yikes!

SAMUEL P. SHELBY – RESUME AFTER YIKES!

Longview, TX | NE Texas | Mobile 999-999-9999 | SShelby69@gmail.com | Hyperlink to Linked In

PROFESSIONAL SUMMARY

Strong relationship seller able to leverage interpersonal friendships for growing sales, gaining market intelligence, and earning 'last look' on opportunities. Expert in bearings and mechanical power transmission solutions. Strives to pull sales through distributors by solving technical or commercial problems that create accountable value.

COMPETENCIES

• Process Industries	• Prospecting, Negotiation & Closing	• Active Listening
• Industrial Distribution & OEM	• Microsoft Office PPT Word Excel	• SAP CRM
• Metals, Paper, Cement	• Selling Through Distribution	• Food & Beverage

EXPERIENCE

BBT Corporation – Longview, TX   12-2018 to 09-2022
Territory Manager – Northeast Texas

- Managed $18M in revenue from OEM (11) , Industrial distributors (16), and end-user accounts (62)
- Set territory goals for sales growth (+8%) and calls (375) and was on plan until Covid19 suspended F2F calls
- Major end user Georgia Pacific, Graphic Packaging, US Steel, Tyson Foods, International Paper, JBS Pilgrim's Pride, Norbord, and Benteler Steel
- Secured first repaired bearing order out of Graphic Packaging in over 3 years
- Won new business worth $1.3M in 2018 and $1.1M 2019

ABC Bearings – Ware, TX   07-2013 to 12-2018
Territory Manager Southwest Region

- Responsible for East Texas, Louisiana, and Arkansas markets valued $7M annually
- Best year over year gain occurred in 2016 with wins in the Oil & Gas, Agriculture, and Food & Beverage markets
- Branch and joint call plans with distributors; Motion Industries, Applied Industrial Technologies, DXP and Purvis
- Provided product training for distributors and end-users

FRED'S INDUSTRIAL SUPERMARKET   *24 years continuous service*

Service Center General Manager – Humble, TX   05-2007 to 06-2017

- Managed a 14-person team generating $12M in revenue and 28% operating income ($5M total budget)
- Articulated and coordinated efforts to support corporate sales and market initiatives getting goals accordingly
- Proactively engaged with customer purchasing and maintenance teams to clearly understand their needs in order to align with premier manufacturers capable of solving commercial or technical problems
- Created a continuous learning program for each employee resulting in a 50% reduction in turnover while ensuring employee compliance
- Developed an aggressive plan to reduce margin leakage through a freight recovery focus which improved profitability by 45 bps (0.45%)
- Serviced the pulp and paper, lumber, food, aggregate, and printing industries

SAMUEL P. SHELBY – RESUME AFTER YIKES!

FRED'S INDUSTRIAL SUPERMARKET   *24 years continuous service*

Outside Sales Representative – Humble, TX   05-1997 to 05-2007

- Built strong working relationships with Georgia Pacific, International Paper, Champion Paper, Tyson Foods, and Pilgrim's Pride in a territory valued at $10M
- Grew business with small and medium accounts to $200K annually for 10 years
- Reported weekly end-user calls, successes and lost sales, while achieving sales plan 8 out of 10 years
- Partnered with premier manufacturers; SKF, Timken, Dodge, Regal Beloit; SealMaster, McGill, Rollway, WEG, Reliance Motors, Flexco, PPI, and Martin Sprocket & Gear

Customer Sales and Service Representative – Dallas, TX   04-1993 to 04-1997

- Worked closely on the phone with customers daily to fill orders and help solve customer problems
- Built strong relationships with customers by taking care of all daily needs in a timely fashion
- In charge of weekly customer order follow-up calls and 'stir' calls designed to promote a new product
- Reviewed back-order reports where we created a follow-up system reducing cancellations 33% saving an estimated $125K in sales annually

EDUCATION

- Texas A & M – College Station, TX
  - Bachelor of Science, Business Administration
  - 3.14 GPA in major
  - Dean's List 5 of 8 semesters

Maggie Simpson - Resume before Yikes!

Maggie Simpson – Before Yikes! Resume

1109 Crooked Highway Apt 312 Birmingham, AL 35242 ■ C: 205-999-0000 ■ MaggieisHot901@gmail.com

Work Experience

Nice Hotel Inn   November 2019 to present
Night Auditor/ Front Desk Agent
Responsible for balancing the revenue and expense transactions averaging $10,000 to $20,000
Maintain overall operations and appearance of the front desk
Interact with guests
Customer Service
Book reservations
Reserve meeting rooms

Southern Womens Athletic Conference   August 2019 to June 2020
Championship Intern
Disseminating pre-championship information to member institutions and staff
Assisting with tournament registration ,coaches meetings and oversee volunteers
Assisting with overseeing the championship assist with awards ceremony
Assist with post-tournament team evaluations and post-tournament reports
Assist with overseeing Hall of Fame process and ceremony
Responsible for ordering and disseminating team gifts and awards
Other duties assigned by the Commissioner.
Ran the social media account
Conduct #SWACChat interviews
Booked all of the interviews
Assist with travel arrangements
Oversea the budget for all events

Sport of Royalty   April 2019 to July 2019
Halftime Coordinator
Coordinator all halftime performances and themes for all home games
Assist with game day promotions

FM 88.7 the Source and 104.1 WHIT Radio   December 2018 to May 2019
Sport Intern
Radio producer/ director of sport events
Edited commerials and interviews
Assisted with the revamp of the station app
Conduct on air interview and book talent for shows

ABC College   August 2018 to December 2018
Properly Assistant (Internship)
Assist with pregame festives
Assist with game day promotions and sponsorships

Education

Master of Science: Sport Management   August 2017 to May 2020
The University of Southern Mississippi **GPA 3.0**
Bachelor of Science: Criminal Justice concentration in Pre-Law   August 2013 to May 2017
Alcorn State
University **GPA 3.4** Cum Laude

References

Winsome McIntosh – General Manager @ Nice Hotel cell (555) 123-1234 email Momma2399@gmail.com
Fred Wilson – Manager @ Sport of Royalty (555) 555-1234 email ManFredW@aol.com
Ms. Simpson – VP Operations @ Southern Womens Athletic Conference cell (555) 555-9999 email VPSWW@SWW.org

Maggie Simpson - Resume after Yikes!

Maggie Simpson – After Yikes! Resume

Birmingham, AL | C: 205-999-0000 | msimpson13@gmail.com |Linked In Profile

CAREER SUMMARY

Reliable, smart, trustworthy, and personable uniquely experienced in higher ed sports, events, and media management. Efficient and energetic communications coordinator able to keep large groups organized, on-time, safe, and aware of their situations. Passionate for sports related enterprises with an emphasis on collegiate level, live sporting event planning, coordination, and execution. Ensures success through proper planning, in-event accessibility, focused communications, and expectation management.

EXPERIENCE

Hilton Hotels, Birmingham, AL   11-2019 to present
Night Auditor / Front Desk Agent
- Responsible and trusted to balance the revenue and expense transactions averaging $10,000 to $20,000 per day
- Maintain overall operations and appearance of the front desk
- Interacts with guests providing their Customer Service experience and perceptions
- Makes reservations, reserves meeting rooms, and addresses special request

All Athletic Conference, Leeds, AL   08-2019 to 06-2020
Championship Intern
- Disseminated pre-championship information to xx member institutions and staff
- Assisted with tournament registration, coaches meetings, and directed and cooridantion of 36 volunteers
- Assisted program manager with the championship celebration and awards ceremony for 502 attendees
- Compiled xx post-tournament team evaluations and post-tournament reports
- Coordinated and oversaw Hall of Fame process and ceremony specializing in award winners and guest satisfaction
- Responsible for ordering and delivering 28 gifts and awards
- Led the social media messaging, conducted "#AACChat" interviews and posted on-line, booked all of the interviews, assisted with travel arrangements, and oversaw the budget for all events
- Adddressed other projects assigned by the Conference Commissioner

Southern Royalty Sports, Hoover, AL   04-2019 to 07-2019
Halftime Coordinator
- Coordinator all halftime performances and themes for x home games
- Assisted with game day promotions; crowd engaging races, sing-a-longs, promotions, and dances

FM 88.7 the Source and 104.1 WHIT News Radio, Montegormery, MS   12-2018 to 05-2019
Sports Radio Internship
- Radio producer/ director of sport events including baseball, basketball, soccer, and football
- Edited commerials and interviews, assisted with the revamp of the station internet application
- Conducted on-air interviews and booked talent for shows

Aubrey College, Laurel, MS   08-2018 to 12-2018
Properly Assistant (Internship)
- Assisted with pregame festivies including game day promotions and sponsor events

EDUCATION

Master of Science: Sport Management
The University of Southern Mississippi **GPA 3.1**
Bachelor of Science: Criminal Justice concentration in Pre-Law
Alcorn State University **GPA 3.4** Cum Laude

Recent College Grad

David L. Smith
Dallas, TX | cell 555.123.1234 | DLSmith202@my.westerntx.edu | Hyperlink to LinkeIn

EDUCATION
UNIVERSITY OF WESTERN TEXAS, Williams College of Business, El Paso, TX

Bachelor's Degree in Business Marketing GPA: 3.67   **05-2021**
- *Graduated Cum Laude, Achieved Dean's List 5 times while a member of the baseball team*
- *3-time Multicultural Academic Award Recipient*
- *Certificate in Advertising (acquired via taking verified rigorous courses)*

EMPLOYMENT
WINGS POWERWASHING, *Business Owner*, El Paso, TX   05-2019 to Present
Founded a business to power wash homes, cars and driveways for the elderly and other people in need of a helping hand
- *Developed and manage a business plan and profit & loss statement and all day-to-day operations*
- *Executed marketing strategies to promote business to target market – elderly and retired people*
- *Established loyal customers by doing what is promised, meeting or exceeding expectations and strong interpersonal skills – notably active listening and processing of needs*

THE HAWK INTERNET RADIO, *Director of Marketing*, Lubbock, TX   01-2021 to 05-2021
- *Created content via Canva for social media platforms, Instagram and Twitter*
- *Created advertising to reach target audience using advanced methods; QR Codes and relatable wording which drove listenership up 26% (in the16-22 year-old demographic)*
- *Interviewed former professional athletes; Mylan Adams – NFL, Ozzie Lamb – MLB*
- *Created, edited, and published weekly blogs for sports programming in WordPress*

WEST TEXAS UMPIRES, *Baseball Umpire*, El Paso, TX   09-2016 to 08-2019
- *Became a state certified umpire for ages 3 to 17*
- *Provided professional services for baseball leagues (ages 3 to 17) promoting safety and core values*
- *Oversaw player safety, sportsmanship, and enforced the code – typically worked 5 games a week*
- *Managed games; conflict resolution, scoring, fines, ejections and counsel, as well as, player performance data*

COMMANDER CODY'S MEDIA, *Social Media Intern*, El Paso, TX   05-2020 to 08-2020
- *Created content for social media platforms designed to reach the upper-middle class clientele on Facebook, Instagram, and Twitter*
- *Achieved novice skill level website builder WordPress, Wix, Milanote, and Weebly with Adobe Stock photos*
- *Interacted with customers and user community using a sense of humor to create a cohesive, powerful content*

EAGLE CREEK OUTFITTERS, *Sales Associate*, Oasis, TX   06-2018 to 05-2019
- *Increased sales by implementing tactics to engage customers and improve overall satisfaction and loyalty – using the Need-Satisfaction method analyzed client needs and provide the best advice for fulfilment*
- *Largest sale was $850 as a result of activity listening to the customer and addressing needs*
- *Coached employees to efficiently complete tasks and enhance the quality of customer interactions by showing an infectious attitude making clients comfortable causing repeat customers.*
- *Organized merchandise with signage and displays marketed to appeal to customer preferences and favorability*

PROFESSIONAL SKILLS
Software: Microsoft Office Suite; Word, Excel, PowerPoint, Business Communication, Social Media Platforms; Twitch, Instagram, YouTube, Twitter, Adobe Premiere
Sales & Marketing: American Marketing Association member, Sports Marketing, Budget Planning, Consumer Behavior, Art of Selling, International Marketing, Cognitive Psychology

EXTRACURRICULAR INVOLVEMENT
UNIVERSITY OF WESTERN TEXAS, *Student Athlete, Men's Baseball Team*   08-2017 to 12-2019
- Played Centerfield and Right Field with a 0.950 fielding rate and 0.301 batting average
- Participated in community events and player appearances to market university athletics
- Motivated team to set and exceed performance goals through effective communication and leadership skills
- Dedicated 4-5 hours daily training while maintaining academic excellence through strong time management skills

Example of a Marketing or Networking Brief

Megan M. Olson | meganolson2023@me.com | iPhone 555-555-1234 | YouTube Link

YouTube Content Creator, Moderator, Actress, & Social Media Personality

Christian faith-based person with exceptional communication skills proven in tutoring, youth counseling, and video

An exceptional communicator with impecable interpersonal skills, comedic sense and timing, with diverse experiences including international teaching and travel. Enthusiasm for live-performance theater, teaching, video performance, and video production. Created and produced a YouTube channel on international travel tips and advice under the stage name "Megan Olson". Prior jobs included Christian Youth Camp Counsler overseeing 10 to 14 campers weekly, 22 hours/day. Campers aged 6 to 18 including foster care and non-English speaking international people. Led campers in spiritual growth, keeping them active, on time, and safe. Online English Teacher of Chinese elementary-age children developed a loyal clientele. Schedule would immediately sell-out at a higher wage-rate. Created YouTube "Tips and Training" courses for apprentice and candidate teachers explaining how to complete training cycles efficiently. Taught in an English Cafe in South Korea. Quickly established a loyal clientele for training sessions. Was recruited to participate by a YouTube streaming channel and contributed on a live-stream cooking show.

GOAL
Communications roles where communication, tutoring, missionary, and performance talents can be showcased in faith based educational and spiritual development programming. On-air show lead, host, or facilitator of training or course work.

PROFESSIONAL EXPERIENCE
- **Online and In-Person Tutor** – Successful in American Sign Language, Elementary Math, and Conversational English
- **Christian Missionary** – Raised $45K to fuel a mission to China reaching xx students with x conversions
- **Waitstaff Server** - Developed a loyal customer base

SKILLS AND INTERESTS ALIGN WITH THESE CHALLENGES
- Teach Christian themed religious material
- Video or voice over production
- Develop programming content with a message
- Produce theater, counseling, or streaming content

EDUCATION & INVOLVEMENT
- University of Mt. Pleasant, Columbus, OH
  - Double Major, Bachelor of Arts in both
  - Middle Childhood Education and Theater
  - Graduated Magna Cum Laude 3.77 GPA (4.00)
  - Best Dramatic Actor 2021
  - Flag-line (Captain)
  - Greek Life Alpha Delta Pi

NOTABLE ROLES
Little Women	Jo March (lead)
Les Miserable	Fantine
Peter Pan	Wendy Darling
Chicago	June
Mulan	Mulan (lead)
Gypsy	Mama Rose (lead)
Beauty and the Beast	Mrs. Potts (co-lead)
Company	April
Charlie Brown	Sally
Into the Woods	Grandma & Giant's Wife
Aladdin	Narrator & Main Dancer

TRADE SKILLS
- Technique, scene study, script analysis, improvisation, cold read, auditioning, self-taping, camera technique
- Singing; Mezzo-Soprano and Alto in musical theater, contemporary, classical styles
- Second Language: American Sign Language (ASL)
- Accents: British, American Southern, Russian,
- Skills: Ukulele, basic keyboard, athletic; bowling, volleyball, tennis, all swimming strokes

Example of a Professional Resume

Mark R. McGyver

Chicago, IL | Cell 555 555-1234 | mcgyv007@gmail.com | LinkedIn Hyperlink

PROFESSIONAL SUMMARY

Highly skilled Automated Machining systems sales professional with +10 years of experience designing custom Cap-Ex systems that most cost-effectively meet project and payback ROI requirements. Expert in understanding which material removal process will be accurate, reliable, and deliver the tolerances and surface finishes required for aerospace, automotive, and complex ultra-precision parts made from the most advanced materials.

EMPLOYMENT HISTORY

CNC Machine Tool Sales   02-2018 to Present
Regional Sales Manager (1099 contractor)

Growing aerospace structural parts sales in Illinois, Iowa, Kansas, Oklahoma and Texas prospecting in the Agricultural, Automotive, and Oil & Gas markets. Responsible for bid and contract negotiations with director level supply chain management. Client requirements included 3, 4 and 5 axis components utilizing CATIA, Cad-Cam 3D modeling software and drawings coordinating closely with manufacturing engineering, upper level procurement and schedulers.

- *Achieved >$1.2M (90%) increase in aerospace RFQ's and sales contracts in first 6 Months*
- *Added >20 new OEM, Tier I & II manufacturing clients*
- *Managed key accounts; Spirit AeroSystems, Lockheed Martin, Boeing Aerospace, John Deere, Textron Aviation, Bombardier, HM Dunn, GKN Aerospace, PCC Aero, Triumph Structures*
- *Recent contract positions include; Precision Products Incorporated and Orco Precision Machine*

Seke Seiki USA – Rosemont, IL   01-2017 to 10-2017
Regional Sales Manager

Recruited to manage $12M pipeline and converted $6.5M in sales via hiring and training factory direct dealer/distributors in Kansas, Oklahoma and Texas. Responsibilities included direct contact and solicitation and Influencing of potential customers, technical product presentations, coordination and preparation of proposals, contract negotiations and closing of orders. Provided annual in class and field product sales training to dealer/distributors. Worked closely with engineers to establish more efficient value-added machining processes to increase client performance and productivity. Recruited dealerships in Oklahoma and Texas.

- *Achieved over $4M in first year sales*
- *Generated 12 projects within the first six months*
- *Managed key accounts; Lockheed Martin, Raytheon, Honeywell Federal, PCC Aero, Figeac Aero*

HHK Mori NA – Chicago, IL   01-2014 to 12- 2016
Area Sales Manager

Hired as the company's first ever factory direct sales engineer responsible for public relations, price negotiations provided innovative machining solutions to customer work requirements on HHK machine tools Promoting the sale of company products and providing technical sales support.

- *Achieved $3.5M in first year sales*
- *Increased supplier classification with John Deere preferred capital equipment supplier through top level management negotiations*
- *Managed local key accounts such as Boeing, Textron, Bombardier Learjet, GKN Aerospace*
- *Received top sales manager awards during first two years with company*

Hilliard MagnaTek Company – Newtown, WI   05-2013 to 01-2014
Inside Sales-Technical Services Consultant

Responsible for maintaining $5M of current business, Account Management, post-sales support, customer service, working with customers and distributors, processing RFQ's utilizing ERP software solutions to manage sales, reviewing blueprints, manufacturing, scheduling and distribution of metal separation products.

Service Sales Engineer   04-2012 to 05-2013
Area Sales Manager (1099 contractor)

Contracted to develop business and expand sales and service in the Midwest United States including customer service, Installation and fabrication for such companies as Tech Weld Automation, C&D Custom Enterprise and Logan Contracting/General Steel Corporation.

Hospitalized and rehabilitated from major auto accident 07-2010 to 04-2012

Creek Electronics Company – Wells Falls, WI   01-2009 to 07-2010
Sales Consultant

Hired as the company's first ever dedicated salesman responsible for outside sales in central states and part of Western Wisconsin and to promote/sell the new TEGG Predictive and Preventative Maintenance Solutions Service.

- *Achieved >$250K first year sales*
- *Produced $170K in new TEGG service program sales*
- *Closed 35% of all working opportunities in the first year*
- *Attained "Preferred Vendor" status with clients; Honeywell Aerospace, Jones Lang LaSalle, GE Engine Services, and LSI Corporation*

Haas Monarch Company – Wichita, KS   02-2008 to 12-2009
Sales Engineer

Recruited to expand sales in Central Kansas and into Western Kansas (position eliminated after only 8 months as a result of an extensive layoff response to the major economic downturn)

Bowen Two Brothers Equipment Company – Wichita, KS   04-2006 to 02-2008
Territory Sales Manager

One of seven Territory Managers in the division. Responsible for Direct Field Sales and Account Management for Central and Southeast Kansas. Demonstrations operating heavy equipment showing equipment efficiencies and capabilities,

- *Recognized as the senior salesperson producing over 30% of heavy equipment sales volume*
- *Increased sales by over 40% sales while maintaining better than 40% gross profit margins*
- *Produced the first ever $1M Territory in division's history in only second year with company*
- *Increased sales volume over 48% in less than 24-months in a historically low producing territory*

Part owner of Midwest Network Solutions which sold refurbished VoIP equipment sold business 12-2001 to 04-2006

The Boeing Company – Wichita, KS   01-1990 to 11-2001
CNC Technician

Assisted with installation/set-up including PLC programming and responsible for troubleshooting, repair, preventative maintenance of conventional and CNC machine tools, machining cells and FMS systems, composite gantry routers, CMM test equipment. Spindle vibration TAP analysis monitoring, cartridge replacement tool retention measurements and repair.

EDUCATION

- Graduate Woburn Classical Vocational Technical Institute – Woburn, MA
- Software Programs - Microsoft Windows, Microsoft Office Word, Excel and PowerPoint
- Sales Force CRM Software
- Microsoft Dynamics CRM Software
- Challenger Sales Training
- Action Coach Sales Training
- CQI-work management & 5-S systems implementation
- Six Sigma Lean Manufacturing
- Kaizen, and JIT/Kanban production methodologies
- GE Fanuc, Siemens and Allen Bradley PLC Controls

Stephen Jones—Industrial Sales before Yikes!

Stephen Jones
Account Manager
555-555-5555 | SWJ 1023@gmail.com | linkedin.com/Stephen-jones101

Professional sales person with 28+ years of experience in the B&PT industry. Combining deep industry knowledge in aggregate, cement, food processing and general manufacturing. Expertise in developing lasting business relationships with customer base and ability to penetrate new accounts.

Skills & Expertise

- Problem Solving
- Time Management
- Mech Drive Design
- Rubber Products (Belting & Hose)
- Negotiation
- Inventory Management
- Fluid Power Experience

Professional Experience

EXPERT TECHNICAL SERVICES, INC. | Denver, CO
Account Manager (Aug 1, 2018 – Aug 2019)
Regional Sales Manager (Nov 2013 – July 2018)

Came into a "green region" with (5) locations of responsibility. During my time as regional manager I helped increase sales from 4.4 million to breaking 9+ million this year.

- Oversaw and rebuilt arrangement of personal to ensure the right people in right positions
- Worked to land agreement with a regional aggregate company through their corporate office
- In current negotiations with another regional aggregate company to sign agreement (this now turned over to corporate)
- Challenged branch managers and their teams to increase GP% as sales increased (5.3% over 4 1/2yrs)

INDUSTRIAL SPECIALITS | Lufkin, TX
General Manager (June 2012 – Oct 2013)
Account Manager (Jan 2015 – June 2012)
Inside Sales (Apr 1994 – Dec 2014)

Hired into location that was doing approximately 1.6 million in sales annually. Was promoted to account manager in 9 months due to customer relationships I was able to build during my time inside. Was able to help increase branch sales to over 4.5 million during my time outside.

- Member of AIT's "A" team for being in top 25 for aggregate sales
- Consistently able to meet required cost savings for corporate contracts
- Oversaw implementation of SAP at local branch

CRESENT MOON INDUSTRIAL SUPPLY | Wichita Falls, TX
Outside Sales (Feb 1991 – Apr 1994)
Warehouse Manager (Jan 1990 – Feb 1991)

Hired as warehouse/delivery driver and was made warehouse manager in 3 months. Company opened store in Graham, TX and offered me an outside sales/store manager position which I did for 4 years before taking opportunity with AIT in Sherman, TX.

Education

ALLAN HANCOCK COLLEGE | SANTA MARIA, CA (1988 – 1989)
General Education Courses

SANTA CRUZ HIGH SCHOOL | SANTA CRUZ, CA (1984 – 1988)

References

Kyle Clausen	BBB/Chrysler Product Manager	555-555-5555	8 years
Missie Angers	Triple J Engineering (Owner)	222-222-2222	24 years
Bob Browner	Joe Mellon Certified Leadership Trainer	555-555-5555	15 years
Brian Gondlier	Quantum Territory Sales Manager	999-999-9999	1 year
Jeremy Henson	Archies Services – Senior Mechanic	444-444-4444	2 years
Jeremy Henson	Alliance Group – Maintenance Manager	444-444-4444	2 years

Example of Optimizing a Resume to a Job Description—Industrial Sales

As indicated in "Step 2: The Resume," your chances of getting a call increases based on the number of keywords and key phrases in your resume that match those listed in the job description. This typically means analyzing the job description and then adding keywords and key phrases into your resume accordingly. You need to optimize your resume for each job description and opportunity you apply for. Below is an example of a before resume optimization and an after resume optimization, which shows how the match percentage increased using www.jobscan.com. This is from my legacy industrial sales career—an area I know well.

The Jobscan.com results showed a 31% match with numerous easy swaps suggested. I was able to create the following resume that achieved "Great" status with an 89% keyword match:

Stephen Jones—Industrial Sales after Yikes! and a keyword match to an industrial sales position.

Stephen W. Jones

Denver CO | Cell 555-555-5555 | swj1023@gmail.com | LinkedIn

PROFESSIONAL SUMMARY

Professional seller with 25 years of success in power generation, oil & gas, aggregate, cement, and food processing industries with MRO and OEM applications. Expert in mechanical power transmission products including bearings, fluid power, conveyor belting, and material handling equipment. Deep product, application, and industry knowledge combined with a tenacious yet friendly consultative, problem-solving approach that creates strong relationships. Builds loyalty *by addressing the customer needs first!*

COMPETENCIES

- Consultative Selling
- Time Management
- Quota Attainment
- Negotiation
- Developing Sellers
- New Account & Bus Dev
- Closing Deals
- Managing Sales Budgets
- Mechanical Drive Design

EXPERIENCE

EXPERT TECHNCIAL SERVICES | Denver CO   10-2013 to 08-2019
Account Manager 08-2018 to 08-2019

- Developed 12 new accounts generating $500K in new sales in 12 months
- Grew assigned accounts from $600K to >$900K (+50%) in revenue while improving gross margins
- Stabilized a branch in transition where leadership turnover added to customer service challenges
- Aligned with key strategic suppliers to execute joint calls focused on creating value for end-users

Regional Sales Manager 11-2013 to 07-2018

Turned around a "green" region with 5 locations leading a sales increase from $4.4M to >$9.0M in five years.

- Oversaw and built a team ensuring the right people were in the right positions
- Closed a $300K agreement with a large aggregate company through ground-up and HQS call strategy
- Challenged branch managers and their teams to increase gross profit percent (total +6%) while doubling sales in less than 5 years
- Grew sales while lowering regional sales headcount from 11 to 7 sellers

INDUSTRIAL SPECIALISTS | Lufkin TX   04-1994 to 10-2013
General Manager 06-2012 to 10-2013 | Account Manager 12-1994 to 06-2012 | Inside Sales 04-1994 to 12-1994

Hired to help turnaround a location worth $1.6M annually then promoted to Account Manager in 9 months. Leveraged customer relationships built while working the order desk. Increased sales to +$4.0M annually.

- Member of "A" team for being in top 25 for aggregate industry sales
- Consistently able to meet required cost savings for corporate 'save or pay' contracts
- Oversaw the implementation of accounting system in the store

CRESCENT MOON INDUSTRIAL SUPPLY | Wichita Falls TX   01-1990 to 04-1994
Warehouse Manager promoted to Outside Sales in February of 1991

EDUCATION

Allan Hancock College | Santa Maria CA
General Education Courses

Sample Cover Letter

Fred Wells
Lumberton, NC

April 11, 2023

Longbow Couplings Company
George Hammaker
VP Sales – Longbow SE Region

Subject: Longbow Coupling Specialist, SE

Hello George,

Please find attached my resume for consideration as a Coupling Specialist for Longbow. I believe my experiences and skills make me a strong fit and well qualified to succeed in the role.

My career has been largely involved selling and servicing the paper and metals markets in sales and in plant roles. This has given my extensive experience in addressing end-user needs and creating accountable value for them. I consistently met or exceeded quotas and expectations. My industrial product sales background is an ideal match to the position requirements.

Position Responsibilities:	Fred Wells - Qualifications:
Sales Territory Management	Utilized my 30+ years of Industrial distribution experience to build a network of relationships with end user Procurement teams, Reliability Engineers, and Manufactures.
Customer Interaction	Identified products aligned with customer's Reliability enhancement objectives. Worked with end-users to integrate those products which generated $3.0M+ in cost savings YOY.
Sales Plan Execution	Managed assigned Strategic Accounts, headquartered throughout North American, with annual sales of $60M+. Actively mentored various account teams with an objective to maximize profit and generate organic growth.
Product Line Extension	Successfully established distributor/manufacture business strategies at all levels (corporate, regional, and local) for an array of Bearing and Mechanical PT products.

I'm confident that my expertise and years of work in distribution sales are uniquely suited for this position with Lovejoy. I look forward to discussing some successful approaches I have experience with and look forward to explaining how they created value. I can be reached by cell phone or text at 555-555-1234 or via email ftwells1234@gmail.com.

Thank you for your consideration,

Fred Wells

Made in the USA
Columbia, SC
26 August 2023